Before I Die Festival in a Box™
How to Hold an End-of-Life Conversation-Starting Event

By Gail Rubin
Certified Thanatologist
& The Doyenne of Death®

First Edition 2023

© Copyright 2023 Gail Rubin
All rights reserved.

No part of this book may be reproduced, stored in a retrieval system, or transmitted by any means, electronic, mechanical, photocopying, recording, or otherwise, without written permission from the author, except in the context of reviews.

Thank you to the Buchanan Group and Private Label caskets for the cover artwork (Timberline model).

Print ISBN: 979-8-9868388-0-9
eBook ISBN: 979-8-9868388-1-6

Published by Light Tree Press
P.O. Box 36987
Albuquerque, NM 87176-6987
www.LightTreePress.com

Praise for the Before I Die Festival in a Box™

"We participate in **Before I Die Festivals** because any time there's a conversation about death and dying, that's where we all need to be. It's a time to gather, a time to meet people from all walks of life. From a funeral home perspective, we also get a chance to have leads that we can follow up in pre-need with families in our communities, so get involved!"

–Tom Antram, President and CEO, French Funerals & Cremations, Albuquerque, New Mexico

"We have great appreciation for our involvement in **Before I Die Festivals**. We found the festival's core mission of educating the public to be consistent with our own mission and values. Removing the mystique around the funeral and cemetery professions – and educating our communities about the value of our services – is time well spent. These festivals can help you teach the importance of honoring a life well lived in a meaningful way. I encourage you to participate in your community."

– Michael Watkins, Vice President, Park Lawn Corporation, Houston, Texas

"I've been a supporter of **Before I Die Festivals** and Gail Rubin's work for many, many years. As the industry has changed, more and more families have become interested in owning their own funeral rituals and participating more. I believe the **Before I Die Festival in a Box** provides an awesome opportunity for funeral directors to really engage with families and start that conversation so that everyone knows what a loved one wants when the time ultimately comes."

– Darren Crouch, President, Passages International, wholesaler of eco-friendly and biodegradable funeral products

"Gail teaches us that a conversation about death is really a conversation about life! The **Before I Die Festival in a Box** is her latest innovation, a step-by-step guide to bring these enlightening conversations to your community. Use this wisdom to create events that inspire your clients to make educated decisions about their own end-of-life plans."

– Seth Viddal, Co-Owner and CEO, The Natural Funeral, Lafayette, Colorado

"**Before I Die Festivals** are vital to help people get comfortable with and plan for the end of life. Gail pours her expertise and passion into this book. Let it be a catalyst to spread the Before I Die movement across the country. Thank you, Gail, for being at the forefront of this important topic. I know I could have never launched our festival without you!"

– Neil Fogarty, Coordinator, **Before I Die Ohio Festival**

To all of those who have planned ahead
for our 100% mortality rate:

Gary Mayhew, I'm looking at you.

Table of

Contents

Foreword by Professor Jenny Kitzinger, Before I Die Festival pioneer 1
Acknowledgments 2
Introduction: We're All Gonna Die! 5
Chapter One: A Short History of Death Discussion Movements 9
  • Why Discuss Death Now? 9
  • Dying Matters 10
  • Death Cafes 11
  • Before I Die Festivals 12
  • Death Over Dinner 13
  • Death Salons and the Death Positive Movement 14
  • Reimagine End of Life Festivals 14
  • Dying to Know Day 15
  • The "Festival" Word 15
Chapter Two: Pandemic-Friendly Festival Formats 17
  • In-Person 17
  • Online 18
  • Hybrid 18
  • Scheduling Events 19

Table of Contents (Continued)

- Unexpected Circumstances 20
- To Charge or Not? 20

Chapter Three: Festival Cost-Sharing Options **23**
- Sponsorships 24
- University Support 25
- Grants 25
- Funding Mechanisms 26
- Typical Festival Expenses 26

Chapter Four: Who's on Your Festival Team? **29**
- Festival Coordinator 29
- Graphic Designer 29
- Online Technical Assistance 30
- Promotion 31
- Database Managers 31
- On-Site Event Managers 32
- Online Services for Ticketing and Surveys 32

Chapter Five: Complementary Business Partners **35**

Chapter Six: Before I Die Festival Topics **41**
- Session Topics 41
- Other Activities 44
- Workshop Ideas 46

Chapter Seven: Before I Die Festival Event Logistics **49**
- Securing Event Locations 49
- Arranging for Speakers 50
- Online Speaker Resources 50
- Festival Video Recordings 52
- Collecting Attendee Information 53
- Mortuary Malls and Behind-the-Scenes Tours 54
- Death Cafes 55
- Before I Die Walls 56
- Post-Event Evaluation and Report 57

Chapter Eight: Mortality Movies and TV Shows **59**
- Films Featuring Funerals and Funeral Directors 59
- TV Shows about Funerals 62

Table of Contents (Continued)

- Movies about Medical Treatment and End-of-Life Issues 63
- Related Movies and Animated Films 65
- Documentaries about Death and End-of-Life Issues 67

Chapter Nine: Marketing Guide **69**
- Planning Approach 69
- Planning Timeline 70
    One Year to Six Months Ahead 70
    Six to Four Months Ahead 70
    Four to Three Months Ahead 70
    Three to Two Months Ahead 71
    Eight Weeks Ahead 71
    Six Weeks Ahead 71
    Four Weeks Ahead 71
    Three Weeks Ahead 72
    Two Weeks Ahead 72
    One Week Ahead 72
    Festival Time 72
    Post-Festival Follow-up 73

Chapter Ten: Sample Before I Die Festival Materials and Forms **75**

Chapter Eleven: More from Gail Rubin **105**
- Before I Die Festival in a Box™ Contents 105
- Film Clip-Illustrated Presentations 106
- Speaking and Consulting 108
- More About Gail 108

Foreword

Death may be feared, but ultimately it cannot be avoided. How we die, and how we live the last years, months, or days of our life, is important. It is important for the individual person, for those who care for and about them, and for the legacy left behind.

This book is an invaluable part of a powerful, multi-dimensional social movement to engage with death and dying. This movement aims to challenge the taboo around talking about death, empower citizens with the information we need, and address the politics, economics, and ethics around the way healthcare, death, and dying are managed.

Crucially, the movement is also about helping people think ahead to ensure that they know what situations await them so they can make decisions now before they have lost the capacity to make decisions for themselves. This is very necessary given that in many countries, including the United States, one in three of us will live the last years of our lives having lost capacity to consent to, or refuse, serious medical treatment.

Death Festivals reclaim death. They are also about fun events and fascinating discussion! Festivals often involve a lot of creativity and laughter as well as lots of information, grief, and sometimes anger.

In this book, Gail Rubin has drawn on her own considerable expertise and collated the experience of others who have run festivals, to create an informative, and imaginative guide to running such events. This wide-ranging book covers the whole process from initial planning to final evaluation and everything in between. It makes helpful suggestions about the range of activities that are possible and the variety of people to engage, from creative artists to healthcare professionals, from community activists to academics.

I also appreciate the pragmatic inclusion of examples of useful paperwork – such as a speaker's release agreement. It is great not to have to reinvent the wheel, but to share such resources so anyone coordinating festivals can get on with the core activity.

Curating a festival about death and dying is a wonderful and challenging process. This book will be an invaluable companion from start to finish.

Professor Jenny Kitzinger,
Cardiff University
Cardiff, Wales, United Kingdom
Before I Die Festival Pioneer

Acknowledgments

Holding a **Before I Die Festival** involves many people, both those who create the event and those who make it possible with their support. Thank you to these people who helped make the **Before I Die Festival in a Box** possible.

The pioneering organizers of **Before I Die Festivals** who helped guide my formation of festival events:
- Professor Jenny Kitzinger, curator of the 2013 Festival in Cardiff, Wales (UK).
- Lucia Wocial, PhD, RN, coordinator of the Indianapolis Festival, April 2016.
- Kel McBride, MLS, CEOLS, a.k.a. the Lively Death Lady, and Justin Magnuson, MA, who, with Deborah Tuggle, MN, APRN, CCNS, FCCM, were the organizers of the **Before I Die Louisville Festival**, October 2016.

To the Intrepids critique group, always amazed at what they learn reading my work: Merilee Dannemann, Joan March, and Donna Pedace.

For those interested individuals who provided feedback on early drafts:
- Garrick Colwell, Kitchen Table Conversations in Austin, TX.
- Mary Ganapol, Arizona End-of-Life Options, Tucson, AZ.
- Jillian Brinkley, Deaconess Health System, Evansville, IN.
- Nancy Klamm, Park Lawn Corporation, Gurnee, IL.
- David Heckel, The Natural Funeral, Lafayette, CO.

Supporters of my early death education work and **Before I Die Festivals**:
- French Funerals & Cremations, Albuquerque, NM.
- Passages International, eco-friendly burial and cremation products, Albuquerque, NM.
- Morris Hall, PLLC, estate planning attorneys, Phoenix, AZ.
- Retirement Extender® financial planning firm, Steve Margulin, CFP,® CMA, ChFC, PFS, CPA.

Thank you also to those companies and organizations that came on board in subsequent years: Daniels Family Funeral Services in Albuquerque, Park Lawn Corporation, National Guardian Life Insurance Company, Compassion & Choices, Estate Pros, LLC, Keeper,™ and many others.

To Linda Hollander for her great guidance on how to get sponsorships.

To Ken Wachsberger, The Book Coach, for editing the manuscript.

And to all the people who have participated in **Before I Die New Mexico Festival** events from 2017 to 2021, both speakers and attendees.

Lastly, eternal appreciation to my husband, David Bleicher, for graphic designing all of my products and supporting our many Doyenne of Death® adventures.

Gail Rubin, CT
Albuquerque, NM

Introduction

We're All Gonna Die!

Even though humans have a 100% mortality rate, fewer than one-third of adults do any end-of-life planning, which includes wills or trusts, advance medical directives, financial planning, and funeral planning. In the 12-plus years since I became a death educator, the number of people who plan has remained stubbornly stuck at this percentage. This leaves roughly 70% of our loved ones scrambling to pull together information and making important and potentially expensive decisions while grieving a death.

Discovering Before I Die Festivals

In 2015, I gave a TEDxABQ talk called "A Good Goodbye." An audience of 1,200 people in Popejoy Hall at the University of New Mexico heard me set a goal to change up the 30% of those who plan to 70% or more. Seven years later, even during a global pandemic, the number of people who plan for end-of-life is still dismally low. Let's face it, funerals are the party no one wants to plan.

However, people are increasingly recognizing the benefits of planning ahead for end-of-life issues. Perhaps it's because the baby boomer generation is seeing more of their contemporaries meet the Grim Reaper and the aftermath when there's been no preparation. Death discussion movements, started in 2010, have blossomed into multiple types of opportunities to start end-of-life planning conversations.

Little did I know during that TEDx talk in 2015 that I would learn about **Before I Die Festivals**. **Before I Die Festivals** give people an attractive way to learn about the many elements of being prepared for death. With a combination of entertainment, education, and discussions, **Before I Die Festivals** put the "fun" in funeral planning. These festivals give people a reason to visit a funeral home or cemetery without having to experience a death in the family.

I held my first **Before I Die Festival** in Albuquerque, New Mexico, October 20-25, 2017. We held 22 events at multiple locations around Albuquerque. Six hundred attendees participated over the six-day festival. A second festival in 2018 drew 685 participants to 32 events in Albuquerque and Santa Fe. The festival expanded to four New Mexico cities in 2019, adding Taos and Espanola. The pandemic forced the event online in 2020, allowing individuals from across the country to participate. The 2021 festival was held as a hybrid online/in-person event in Albuquerque.

Over the course of five years, these **Before I Die Festival** events in New Mexico have directly addressed many topics about which people have questions. We've had speakers and panels on life after death, medical aid-in-dying in New Mexico, estate and financial planning, advance medical directives, pre/post-death downsizing, grief issues, and history and culture surrounding death. Authors on related topics discussed their books. We've gone behind-the-scenes at funeral homes, crematoria, prep rooms, and cemeteries. We held panel discussions with funeral directors from different funeral homes, including the pub-based "Millennial Morticians with ABQ Brews."

In 2018, the International Cemetery, Cremation, and Funeral Association (ICCFA) recognized the **Before I Die New Mexico Festival** with the KIP (Keeping It Personal) Award for Best Event. In 2022, *The Wall Street Journal* featured the festival movement in a story on November 3, 2022, titled "How Morticians Are Putting the Fun in Funerals."

Here's how festival participants described their experiences:
- "Thanks for making death easy to talk about! The festival had a wide range of topics and was a great learning experience!"
- "I loved the upbeat nature of the presentations and the sensitivity of the speakers."
- "The **Before I Die Festival** is an informative, inclusive, and creative event that is even fun! Very helpful!"
- "This is an excellent way to find out about various topics in just a few days, all packaged together."

- "I attend many events within the funeral/cemetery profession. I found the **Before I Die Festival** to be very informative – with a variety of topics that are not common among the events I normally attend. Having recently lost my mom, I did get some valuable takeaways both regarding her estate as well as how to work on preparing my own!"
- "This festival has something for EVERYONE who is interested in end-of-life issues. Great speakers, great topics, great opportunities for participation."
- "Gail has a way of bringing the topic of death and dying to life in a most enjoyable way!"

If we are to help start preneed conversations on a bigger scale, we need more communities to hold **Before I Die Festivals**. Individuals have approached me about how they can hold their own festivals in their markets. After five consecutive years of holding festivals, I've got some wisdom to share.

Dying to Know Who I Am?

Some background about me: Before becoming a Certified Thanatologist – a fancy name for a death educator, I was a public relations professional and event planner. After a fun, creative Jewish Western wedding for my second marriage, I wanted to write a book about creative life cycle events and call it "*Matchings, Hatchings and Dispatchings*."

While writing a monthly newspaper feature by that name, focused on weddings, births, and deaths, I discovered that the stories about death and funerals got the most reader response. There are plenty of books on creative wedding planning, but 15 years ago, there were few about creative funeral planning. I focused on funerals, and it changed the course of my career.

As The Doyenne of Death,® I use humor, film and video clips, and outside-the-box activities to teach about death, funeral planning, and preparing for end-of-life issues. A doyenne is a woman considered senior in a group who knows a lot about a particular subject. I'm also an award-winning speaker, a Certified Funeral Celebrant, and a licensed life insurance agent in New Mexico.

My books and products include
- *A Good Goodbye: Funeral Planning for Those Who Don't Plan to Die.*
- *Hail and Farewell: Cremation Ceremonies, Templates, and Tips.*
- *Kicking the Bucket List: 100 Downsizing and Organizing Things to Do Before You Die.*
- *Newly-Dead® The Game* – a fun way to quiz couples and individuals on end-of-life topics.
- *The Family Plot File* – an electronic data management resource.

In addition to becoming an expert on holding **Before I Die Festivals**, I became one of the first people to hold a Death Cafe in the United States in 2012. You'll find out more about the Death Cafe movement in Chapter One, "A Short History of Death Discussion Movements"; and how to put on your own Death Cafe in Chapter Seven, "Before I Die Festival Event Logistics."

The **Before I Die Festival in a Box** gives you the tools and guidance you need to hold your own successful festival. Whether you run a funeral home, cemetery, or related end-of-life business, or just want to bring this kind of event to your community, thank you for helping to educate people on planning ahead for our 100% mortality rate.

Chapter 1

A Short History of Death Discussion Movements

Funeral directors and cemeterians recognize that most people are not eager to discuss end-of-life issues. Yet, there are thousands of people who want to discuss death. You can see it in the remarkable worldwide rise of death discussion movements since 2009.

The most popular death discussion movements got started in the United Kingdom. These include Dying Matters Awareness Week held every May, Death Cafes, and **Before I Die Festivals**. People in the United States can take credit for starting Death Over Dinner, Death Salons, and Reimagine End of Life Festivals.

Why Discuss Death Now?

Why are people taking death out of the closet to speak openly of mortality issues now? The parade of life has moved much of the Silent Generation, those born between 1928 and 1945, into the grave. This group is also called the Traditionalist Generation, known for "working within the system."

Baby boomers, those born between 1946 and 1964 during the post-World War II baby boom, are next in line. This Silver Tsunami of 76 million Americans are all about "changing the system." The Census Bureau projected that the baby boom population will total 61.3 million in 2029, when the youngest boomers reach age 65.

Baby boomers are aging and dying. But the generation that celebrated sex, drugs, and rock n' roll is determined to change the end-of-life script. They don't want the traditional funerals they may have experienced for their grandparents or parents. This attitude drives an openness to discussing death. There is still great resistance to talking about end-of-life issues, but the rise of these death discussion movements shows attitudes are changing.

While **Before I Die Festivals** appeal to some curious folks in younger generations, the baby boomer demographic comprises 75% of attendees at festivals I've held. The vast majority of participants are women.

People will start end-of-life planning conversations if approached in a non-salesy way. They want to be educated while being entertained. Demographer Kenneth W. Gronbach explained it this way: "My long-standing axiom for selling to Boomers is: *Make my life easy. Save me some time. Don't rip me off.*" **Before I Die Festival** events can help open doors to planning *before* there's a death in the family.

The worldwide pandemic accelerated the urgent need to plan and elevated the visibility of death and preneed end-of-life planning. When the coronavirus pandemic shut down much of the world in March 2020, many death discussion movements pivoted to holding online-only events. More than two years later, as restrictions have loosened up, events are being held again in-person, often offered with an online hybrid component.

Dying Matters

In 2009, the National Council for Palliative Care (NCPC) set up the Dying Matters Coalition to promote public awareness of dying, death, and bereavement among the citizens of the United Kingdom (U.K.). The National Health Service England and Hospice UK eventually took over funding and coordinating the effort.

Dying Matters encourages people to talk with friends, family, and loved ones about wishes regarding the end of their lives, including where they want to die and their funeral plans. Every year in May, Dying Matters and their coalition members host an Awareness Week, an opportunity to place the importance of talking about dying, death, and bereavement firmly on the national agenda. The first event in 2010 featured just a handful of events.

Dying Matters has grown dramatically. In 2018, Dying Matters Week ran from May 14 to 20, with more than 500 events and 10,000 participants in England, Wales, and Scotland. Events included speakers and panel discussions, Death Cafes, theatre performances, field trips to anatomy labs, funeral homes, cemeteries, and other related places, grief resources, art shows, and more. Dying Matters Week inspires multiple news stories that can help raise awareness about preneed funeral planning.

Dying Matters Week has used an open-source approach to list any event that can be considered relevant. An online form allows individuals or organizations to schedule an event to be included under the Dying Matters umbrella. Check their website to see how events are currently curated: **www.HospiceUK.org/our-campaigns/dying-matters**.

Death Cafes

The Death Cafe movement started in England in September 2011, when Jon Underwood and psychologist Sue Barsky Reid, his mother, held the first such event in the basement of Jon's London home. Jon was inspired by the work of Swiss sociologist Bernard Crettaz, whose *Café Mortel* events enabled participants to discuss death while drinking coffee and eating pastries.

The Death Cafe objective is "to increase awareness of death with a view to helping people make the most of their (finite) lives." The sessions offer a group-directed discussion of death with no agenda, objectives, or themes. They are a discussion group rather than a grief support or counseling session. One Death Cafe cornerstone is the offering of cake or cookies, coffee or tea, or other nourishing snacks to support what can be a difficult conversation.

Death Cafes are a "social franchise," where those who want to hold such events under the Death Cafe name agree to follow uniform guidelines. The guidelines include presenting Death Cafes on a not-for-profit basis in an accessible, respectful, and confidential space, with no intention of leading people to any conclusion, product purchase, or course of action. Most Death Cafes are free or held on a donation basis.

Prior to the pandemic, hosts always offered refreshments as part of the Death Cafe experience. The events were held in cafes, restaurants, libraries, funeral homes, cemeteries, and other places where people could gather to eat, drink, and talk.

In March 2020, lockdowns prompted Death Cafe hosts to pivot to online discussions, most taking place over Zoom. One benefit of online events is the elimination of geographic barriers. People in different states and countries can participate in an online Death Cafe.

From the first event in 2011 to November 2022, more than 15,100 Death Cafes have been held in 82 countries around the world. Lizzy Miles and I held the first two U.S. Death Cafes in 2012, in Columbus, Ohio, and Albuquerque, New Mexico, respectively.

In a cruel irony, Jon Underwood died unexpectedly at the age of 44 on June 27, 2017 from a brain hemorrhage caused by undiagnosed leukemia. His mother, Sue Barsky Reid, and sister, Jools Barsky, continue to run the movement's website, **www.DeathCafe.com**.

In 2013, death discussion movements exploded on the public scene, with **Before I Die Festivals**, Death Salons, and Death Over Dinner events.

Before I Die Festivals

Like the Death Cafe movement, **Before I Die Festivals** originated in the United Kingdom. **Before I Die Festivals** boldly take death out of the closet through a host of entertaining and engaging free or low-cost activities. These events help participants to think about, talk about, and plan for our eventual mortality.

The first **Before I Die Festival** was held in 2013 at Cardiff University in Wales, in the United Kingdom. The curator of the events was Professor Jenny Kitzinger. Her research focuses on the treatment of patients in comas and what are sometimes called "right-to-die issues" — although Jenny always stressed this is actually about "the right to not be subjected to unwanted life-sustaining treatment."

A second festival was held in 2014 at the University of York, with 700 attendees over a week. Both festivals were part of a network of events held across the U.K. for Dying Matters Week. A video interview with Professor Kitzinger about how she curated the first festival is available on YouTube, titled "**Before I Die Festival** How-To Interview: Jenny Kitzinger." You can also find it on the blog at **www.BeforeIDieFestivals.com**.

After 2014, no one held another **Before I Die Festival** until the University of Indiana School of Nursing received a grant to hold one on April 15-17, 2016. The festival was scheduled to align with National Healthcare Decisions Day on April 16. Yes, let's talk about Death and Taxes! In Indianapolis, 800 people attended 28 activities over three days.

The second U.S. **Before I Die Festival** was held in October 2016 in Louisville, Kentucky. Coordinators were Kel McBride, the Lively Death Lady of Clearly Depart; Justin Magnuson, a death educator, hospice volunteer, and Death Cafe host; and Deb Tuggle, a clinical nurse specialist with Critical Care Consultants. Their first festival drew over 700 people to 17 events over the course of a month. Festival events were also held in 2017 and 2018 with the support of community collaborators. Their website is **www.BeforeIDieLou.com**.

Kel McBride said of their festival in Louisville, "My focus through all of this is to get younger, healthier people to make a plan, because I'm very aware about one in four of us don't make it to 65. Yet we tend to think of death as planning for something you don't worry about until you're older.... So, engaging people in a fun way, you have to do that to engage that 20- to 55-year-old audience group."

Justin talked about the benefits of teaming with organizations to create programming. "You don't want to talk someone into doing something they don't want to do. But if there's some kind of chemistry.... If people go to church every Wednesday evening, and they already have a built-in audience, you can ask if they would introduce this as a topic of discussion. That's much better than saying, 'I'm going to take this topic and try and do it all myself.'"

You can see a conversation with Kel and Justin about their insights on putting a festival together. They talk about creative festival ideas, challenges they faced, and advice for people who may want to hold a festival. It's on YouTube as "**Before I Die Festival** How-To Interview: Justin Magnuson and Kel McBride" and on the blog at **www.BeforeIDieFestivals.com**.

The first U.S. **Before I Die Festival** west of the Mississippi was held on October 20-25, 2017, with 22 events held at multiple locations around Albuquerque. This festival was supported by sponsors and coordinated by yours truly, Gail Rubin. Six hundred attendees participated over the six-day festival. A second festival in 2018 drew 685 participants to 32 events. The festival expanded to four New Mexico cities in 2019, then went totally online in 2020. The 2021 festival was held as a hybrid online/in-person event in Albuquerque. **www.BeforeIDieFestivals.com**.

Funeral homes in El Paso, Texas, and Bakersfield, California, have held one-day **Before I Die Festivals** on-site that drew good crowds and generated preneed sales that provided great return on investment. The first **Before I Die Ohio Festival** was held October 27-29, 2022, in Dayton, Ohio.

Death Over Dinner

The Death Over Dinner movement launched in the United States on August 24, 2013, with over 500 dinners in 20 countries on a single night. Since then, there have been more than 100,000 #deathdinners around the globe. A Death Over Dinner event can be a great addition to a **Before I Die Festival**.

It started with a University of Washington graduate course called Let's Have Dinner and Talk About Death, taught by Michael Hebb and Scott Macklin. They recognized that how we end our lives is the most important and costly conversation America is NOT having.

The project provides a simple set of tools to help families and friends address the fact that we are all, at some point, going to die. We suffer more when we don't communicate our wishes; we suffer less when we know how to honor the wishes of our loved ones. The online platform has different versions for specific demographics: a Jewish Edition, a Healthcare Edition, and for Americans, Australians, and Brazilians.

Michael Hebb's book, *Let's Talk About Death Over Dinner*, provides a practical guide to holding these difficult conversations over the comforting ritual of breaking bread. Tools are also available at **www.DeathOverDinner.org**.

Death Salons and the Death Positive Movement

Caitlin Doughty is a mortician, activist, funeral industry rabble-rouser, *New York Times* bestselling author, and star of the popular YouTube series, "Ask a Mortician." In 2011, she founded the death acceptance collective, The Order of the Good Death, and coined the term "death positive."

She is the moving force behind Death Salons,® "events that bring together intellectuals and independent thinkers engaged in the exploration of our shared mortality by sharing knowledge and art." They "aim to subvert death denial by opening up conversations with the public about death and its anthropological, historical, and artistic contributions to culture."

The first Death Salon event was held in Los Angeles in October 2013. Other sold-out Death Salon events were held annually in diverse locales, including Seattle, London, San Francisco, Houston, and Boston. Death Salons ceased being held in 2018 and have yet to be revived. Individuals are encouraged to hold their own death discussion events, but to avoid calling them Death Salons as "Death Salon" is a trademarked name and unauthorized use of the name will be prosecuted as trademark infringement. More information can be found at **www.DeathSalon.org**.

Reimagine End of Life Festivals

Reimagine End of Life is a nonprofit organization that hosts public conversations exploring life and death, living life to the fullest, and preparing for the time when we won't be here anymore. Reimagine started in 2016 as a prototype of OpenIDEO's End of Life Challenge. Their Challenge was part of an effort to investigate the intersection of art, community, and end of life.

The inaugural Reimagine End of Life festival in San Francisco offered 175 free and paid events all around the Bay Area between April 16 and 22, 2018. Events included art shows, film screenings and theater performances, speakers and field trips, workshops and panel discussions, and concerts. They estimate more than 10,000 attendees participated over the course of the festival.

Another festival took place in New York City from October 27 to November 3, 2018, and it drew similarly impressive numbers. They planned to expand the number of these festivals to multiple markets in the United States. Reimagine brought the **Before I Die Festival** concept to a previously unachieved level of engagement.

In 2020, the pandemic brought these in-person events to a screeching halt. The organization pivoted to hold a series on ongoing online events, including Death Cafe discussions, theater, art, yoga, panel discussions, and special speakers. The organization reviews and approves the individuals and organizations that can hold events and offer resources. In September 2022, Reimagine re-started in-person events while continuing online events. Learn more at **www.LetsReimagine.org**.

Dying to Know Day

Another death discussion movement in the English-speaking world is Dying to Know Day in Australia and New Zealand. This annual campaign held every year on August 8, during their wintertime, empowers people at all stages of life to live and die well. Events take place over the course of the month, and individuals are invited to register their own events. Learn more at **www.DyingtoKnowDay.com**.

As the infections and deaths from the COVID-19 pandemic ebb and in-person events return, we will likely still see online options for death discussion events continue. You may find aspects of these death discussion movements to be helpful in creating your own **Before I Die Festival**.

The "Festival" Word

A word about calling a death discussion event a festival. Hospices can be great partners for a **Before I Die Festival**. However, hospices are sensitive to the use of the word "festival." The top definition of the word is "a day or period of celebration marked by special observances…" Also "gaiety, conviviality."

Hospices deal with death and dying daily. They seek to provide comfort care to the patient and support for the patient's loved ones. A person can go on hospice care with a diagnosis of a medical condition projected to be terminal within six months. Some people live for months or even years on hospice care. All too often, patients see hospice as a last resort and die within hours or days of discharge from a hospital.

You can only laugh about death when it seems like a distant possibility. Part of the attraction of a festival is reducing the fear of death and talking about its impact on individuals and their families. If the word "festival" in the title of your death discussion event scares off hospice participation, you can consider calling the event something else.

You could call the event **Before I Die (City or State)** and leave off the word "Festival." Other options to consider:
- **Before I Die (City or State) Events**
- **Before I Die (City or State) Expo**
- **Before I Die (City or State) Project**
- **Before I Die (City or State) Experience**
- **Before I Die (City or State) Undertaking**.

As a participant in the **Before I Die Festival** movement, your events can be listed and shared online through the calendar of events at the website, **www.BeforeIDieFestivals.com**.

Chapter 2

Pandemic-Friendly Festival Formats

Before the coronavirus pandemic, no one questioned the idea of meeting in the flesh for festival events. In-person events at specified locations were the default assumption. Coronavirus changed all that starting in March 2020. As pandemic restrictions fade, people are returning to in-person events, while being open to online and hybrid in-person/online events.

Even as coronavirus vaccines made a return to in-person events possible in 2021, unpredictable waves of infection may hamper an ongoing return to normalcy. We don't know if another pandemic is waiting in the wings. We need to be flexible with how we hold events going forward, whether using an in-person, online, or hybrid approach.

In-Person

People like to meet in-person. They can more easily share stories, ask questions, and feel part of something bigger than themselves. After more than two years of pandemic living, people are just tired of Zoom meetings.

Where could you hold your event? Get creative! Consider libraries, movie theaters, art studios, university continuing education centers, funeral homes, cemeteries, houses of worship, and community centers. You may be able to rent these locations for free or a minimal cost. Invite businesses and organizations to be in-kind sponsors and promote their support of your festival.

Avoid holding a festival at places that will cost a lot of money such as hotels, resorts, or event centers. While assisted living centers might seem like a logical place to hold events, it's hard to laugh about and discuss planning for death when the Grim Reaper visits these places on a regular basis. If holding events outdoors, have a Plan B for a sheltered location in case of inclement weather.

Another consideration is transportation to events. Is there abundant parking and/or access to good public transportation? Avoid holding events in crime-ridden areas of town where participants might be uncomfortable visiting.

Online

During the early days of the pandemic lockdown, the Reimagine End of Life Festival (**www.LetsReimagine.org**) pivoted to holding their events totally online. What started with very large in-person festival events in the San Francisco Bay Area and in New York City evolved to multiple online events.

After three years of holding in-person events, I debated whether to hold the fourth annual Before I Die New Mexico Festival in 2020. With about four months of planning, I went ahead with an online series of events over four days, and it worked well. My local IT person facilitated the online sessions on Zoom.

If you are holding online events, have a technical support person to make sure the sessions run smoothly. You should also have each presenter spend about 30 minutes in online rehearsal prior to the festival. Rehearsals would include your event host and your tech person to make sure any audio-visual components, such as PowerPoint slides or videos, work as envisioned.

There are numerous companies that can facilitate online festivals. I have worked with GatheringUs, Keeper,™ and Whova. Charges for the use of their services can vary based on the number of participants, how many days or events you plan, and how fancy you want to get with online networking, message boards, and other features. You may be able to negotiate with a provider to become a festival partner. In exchange for their services, they are promoted along with the festival sponsors.

In late 2022, Keeper acquired GatheringUs. The company specializes in virtual and hybrid memorial service events, as well as free online memorials and tributes. Learn more at **www.MyKeeper.com**.

Hybrid

In 2021, with the help of GatheringUs, the **Before I Die New Mexico Festival** was held with two days of in-person/online hybrid events and two days of primarily online events with in-person evening events. The hybrid in-person/online approach enabled us to have the best of both worlds.

With people gathered in-person, guest speakers from across the country addressed the audience in the room as well as those joining online from other markets. For those events that were held solely in-person, we video recorded the speakers and made videos of those sessions to share online after the festival was over.

Technical considerations for a hybrid event include the following:
- Have one or more large-screen monitors with speakers in the room, so in-person participants can see and hear the people joining in from afar.
- Make sure there's a high-speed internet connection at the in-person location.
- Use an external video camera and microphone connected to a laptop computer to provide a high-quality video and audio feed to the virtual participants. Built-in laptop cameras and microphones are generally less than top quality.
- Have the host repeat comments from the in-person audience into the microphone so online participants can clearly hear the questions.
- Engage the services of a professional to make sure technical considerations you haven't thought of are handled well.

There are different ways to hold hybrid events. Many hybrid events are held on Zoom; other options include Facebook Live and a variety of online platforms.

Scheduling Events

There are two approaches to scheduling festival events. You can schedule one event at a time, so participants don't have to choose one event over another. Or you can schedule multiple events at the same time, which can cause people to complain about having to miss one session while attending another. If you want to accommodate more attendees at a one-day event, you can repeat certain sessions to deflect scheduling conflict issues.

At the first U.S. **Before I Die Festival** in Indianapolis, the events overlapped and participants had to choose which events they would attend. "People complained because they didn't want to miss anything," said Lucia Wocial, the festival coordinator.

Recording sessions and sharing videos of those sessions online is a great way to preserve and extend the reach of the information shared in festival events. Recognizing festival sponsors in video recordings provides a continuing benefit for sponsors as well as partners.

Unexpected Circumstances

The Perches Funeral Homes in El Paso, Texas, arranged to hold a one-day **Before I Die Festival** on August 17, 2019, at one of their locations which included the El Paso Funeral Museum. On August 3, two weeks before the festival was to be held, a mass shooting took place at a Walmart in El Paso, killing 22 and injuring many others.

The last funeral was held on August 16 at Perches' La Paz Faith Center. The event drew national media coverage. One thousand flower arrangements were sent by well-wishers from across the country and around the world. Thousands of people waited in the summer heat to pay their respects. Read the full story at **https://agoodgoodbye.com/field-notes/witness-to-the-el-paso-strong-weekend/**.

A mass shooting changes the circumstances around death discussion. It was hard to laugh and learn about death while this grim reality affected the entire community. The festival schedule was changed to include a second Death Cafe discussion opportunity, and a session about grief and mourning was added. Attendees appreciated these program changes. It's important to be flexible in the face of unexpected circumstances.

To Charge or Not?

Should you charge participants a fee to attend? When holding in-person events the first three years of **Before I Die New Mexico Festivals**, I did not charge a fee and relied on sponsorship funding to cover the costs. When events shifted online during the pandemic, many event organizers found that people would register for free online events but not show up.

For the online **Before I Die New Mexico Festival** in 2020, I offered four levels of tickets:
- One-day passes for $20
- A pass for just theater/film events or only Death Cafe conversations for $20
- A four-day pass for $50
- A VIP Experience pass for $100 for all events plus a box of goodies mailed to the participant's home.

Depending on the investment, participants were sent different Zoom links. This made the online registration unnecessarily complicated. Even with the financial investment, some people still did not show up for online events. The post-festival videos helped those individuals who wanted to get their money's worth and see what they missed. All festival programs were recorded, except for the Death Cafe discussions, which are confidential.

In 2021, with the hybrid in-person/online model, I asked attendees for donations of $25, $50, $100, or whatever they could afford. Registration donations ranged from $4 to $100. Most people appreciate the work that goes into creating a **Before I Die Festival** and want to provide some financial support. The entire online portion of the festival was held through one Zoom link, making participation much easier for the attendees, the presenters, and the organizers.

Food at events can be a large expense that needs to be covered. You can make most festival events free and only charge for a special dinner or all-day symposium where meals will be provided. Partnering with a caterer or grocery store to donate meals is another option.

More about sponsors and financing your festival in the next chapter!

Chapter 3

Festival Cost-Sharing Options

Holding a successful **Before I Die Festival** requires some financial resources. The most basic out-of-pocket costs can include advertising, printing materials, the services of virtual assistants, postage, food and drink, and gifts for speakers and sponsors. How can you make festival events widely available and not lose money? Find ways to bring in funds.

Consider what businesses would benefit from connecting with the audience that will be attracted to festival events. Most attendees at the five **Before I Die NM Festivals** I coordinated were women baby boomers. The second largest demographic is millennials, the children of baby boomers. What end-of-life related businesses would want to connect with these audiences?

Your approach may depend on who is putting this festival together: a funeral home or cemetery, another end-of-life-related business, a nonprofit organization, or an individual.

For funeral homes, cemeteries, and other end-of-life businesses, consider festival expenses as a part of your advertising budget. The festival also offers public relations opportunities to connect with complementary businesses in your community and generate positive news media coverage.

Funeral homes or cemeteries can invite local financial planners, estate planning attorneys, hospice representatives, Death Cafe hosts, death doulas, authors, banks or credit unions, and news media to participate in panel discussions or as featured speakers. For financial support, funeral homes might approach the insurance companies or trust organizations that fund preneed funeral arrangements. A funeral home might partner with companies that market preneed funeral planning. If you have a preneed planning counselor or staff, they might be charged with organizing the event, as a festival can lead to many sales opportunities afterward.

Sponsorships

For those individuals or nonprofit organizations seeking to create a local festival, these same end-of-life businesses can be sponsors. They can provide valuable cash or in-kind services. To get sponsorships, you need to know the demographics of your target audience and have a proposal that outlines the benefits of being a **Before I Die Festival** sponsor.

Linda Hollander, CEO of Sponsor Concierge, has mentored hundreds of people on how to achieve success with sponsors. "Most people don't reach their big dreams because they have a lack of capital. Sponsorship takes care of that," she explained. "You need to ask for enough money to pay yourself, for contingency expenses, and money in the bank for your next event."

And give yourself plenty of lead time to look for sponsors – eight months to a year. "Sponsorship is a relationship business, and it takes time to form those relationships. You have to get your proposal done, put up a good-looking website, and create your promotion campaigns," she said.

You can get Linda Hollander's #1 Secret for Getting Sponsors and free sponsor tips at **www.SuccessWithSponsors.com**. You can also see a YouTube video interview with Linda about sponsorships for **Before I Die Festivals** titled "Linda Hollander on Sponsorships." It's also available in a blog post at **www.BeforeIDieFestivals.com**.

Your sponsor proposal needs to be written in a way that emphasizes the benefits for the sponsors: to connect them to their target audience, raise awareness of their products and services, and generate sales. Tell stories of those who want to discuss death and have benefitted from interactions with you as the coordinator of the festival. Use colorful photographs and meaningful quotes from participants. Let sponsors know your experience and why you are the best person to make this festival happen.

For more information on obtaining sponsorships, you'll find a sample sponsor proposal for holding a festival at the back of the book. The example is my sponsorship proposal for the **Before I Die New Mexico Festival**. You can model the content of your proposal to reflect your unique qualifications, the marketing benefits you provide, your marketing plans supported by numbers, program details, a charitable partner, and the benefits packages in several levels of sponsorships.

You may need to adjust your funding level requests to be appropriate for your market. But don't sell yourself short! Start with a bigger number and negotiate down if you need to. A festival partner can provide in-kind services including a venue for events, local advertising placements or news media coverage, food donations, and printing.

University Support

The first **Before I Die Festival** was held in 2013 in Cardiff, Wales, in the United Kingdom. The curator of the events was Professor Jenny Kitzinger, whose research focuses on the treatment of patients in comas and right-to-die issues.

Professor Kitzinger's university provided her with an intern who helped implement the programs, public relations support from the communications department, and students who conducted the festival evaluation survey as a school project. Most out-of-pocket costs involved photocopying materials. This kind of support from a university can be priceless.

You can also team up with the continuing education programs at many universities. These programs can list the festival as an upcoming event in their catalogue of programs, provide facilities to hold events, and use their registration system to collect information on attendees.

Grants

As noted earlier, the first U.S. **Before I Die Festival** was held by the University of Indiana School of Nursing in Indianapolis. The school got a grant to hold a three-day event tied to April 16, Healthcare Decisions Day. Playing on the theme of death and taxes, this grant paid for the first U.S. **Before I Die Festival**.

Most grant organizations require that the funding recipient be a nonprofit organization. It's possible for an individual to team up with a local nonprofit to secure grant funding for a festival. Before applying for a grant or a sponsorship, you'll need at least a six-month lead time, an idea of what you want to do, and a complete budget estimate.

A report on how the money was spent and achievements is usually a requirement for grant funding. If working with sponsors, provide them with this same information so they can see the benefits of their investment.

Funding Mechanisms

How can you accept payments for festival events? You can choose from several low-cost options that don't require complicated and expensive online payment gateways. I have used PayPal, Square, and Stripe linked to a bank account to accept payments, create tickets, and track sales.

You are not assessed any ongoing charge to use these services. They charge a per-transaction fee based on a percentage of the amount charged. Fees can range from 1.5% to 4% of the payment amount.

Online shopping cart programs can be used on your festival website to manage registrations. Work with an IT person to pick the best one for your purposes. Make sure your registrants are automatically added to an email list for ongoing communications after they sign up.

Event or conference apps that allow you to manage registrations and attendee communications may also offer ways to collect funds. Free and paid versions of apps offer a wide range of options for in-person, hybrid, and online event management.

Typical Festival Expenses

Festival out-of-pocket expenses can include
- printing costs for event flyers, brochures, and postcards
- postage for mailing materials
- advertising placements in traditional and social media
- photocopying
- supplies (labels, envelopes, gift bags)
- swag items and gifts
- refreshments at events
- gifts for speakers and sponsors
- outdoor banners and indoor signage.

Expenses for services can include technical support, public relations, video production, survey fees, and data entry. If you travel to different markets to hold events, hotels and meals are another expense.

Should you pay for speakers? You may find that many local professionals in end-of-life businesses will speak for free, as a marketing opportunity. You can find a listing of interesting speakers, both virtual and in-person, at **www.BeforeIDieFestivals.com**.

One cost I hope you will avoid is for your event location. I mentored a woman who wanted to hold a **Before I Die Festival** in her city. She had a grand vision of attracting hundreds of people who would pay big bucks to listen to speakers and visit with exhibitors at a resort hotel. I counseled against that approach. The hotel she contracted with was going to charge $40,000 for the use of the facilities. In addition, if she cancelled, she would still be charged $20,000.

While she lined up a great slate of speakers and a wonderful group of exhibitors, the paying attendees did not materialize in huge numbers. She cancelled at the resort a week before the event and was able to get a last-minute deal at another hotel. Still, she lost a great deal of money by not following my advice. Find venues that are free or at least not much money!

Hosting events at funeral homes and cemeteries can be a part of a sponsorship package as a benefit to those businesses. Funeral homes, as well as many cemeteries, have reception centers and chapels which make great locations to hold in-person **Before I Die Festival** events.

Behind-the-scenes tours are fascinating to the general public. They want to know about the cremation process. It's an opportunity to share information about the many options now available in funerals and memorial services. Those establishments that are adept at hybrid in-person/streaming services can use those skills for speakers and panel discussions, reaching people who can't or don't want to attend in person.

Chapter 4

Who's on Your Festival Team?

It takes a team to successfully hold a **Before I Die Festival**. During the first years as the coordinator of the **Before I Die Festival** in New Mexico, I was a one-person show. I was exhausted. Plus, it's risky to be the sole key person on a project. If the festival coordinator fell off the face of the planet, who would carry out the work of making the festival happen?

Even in the early years, other people helped facilitate festival events. You need time to plan as well, at least three to six months ahead of the event. Here are key festival roles to fill.

Festival Coordinator

The festival coordinator oversees creating the flow of events; arranging for venues to host events; contacting speakers, sponsors, and partners; scheduling the presentations and events; and deciding what will take place in-person, online, or hybrid. It helps to have a paper calendar to map out all the moving parts. Once key parts of the event are set, you can begin to promote the festival.

Graphic Designer

To create eye-catching marketing materials, you'll need the services of a graphic designer. These elements can include postcards, brochures, flyers, ads, posters, website art, and even the drawing slips to collect information. I'm blessed that my husband Dave is a graphic designer. He's my go-to person for these important elements, and he works for food.

Canva.com is a free-to-use online graphic design tool. It can be used to create social media posts, presentations, posters, videos, logos, and more. You can also do an online search for "free online graphic design software." You may want to hire someone or find someone willing to donate their time and talents, depending on your budget.

If you have the budget to work with an ad agency or PR firm, they can help with a multitude of marketing elements: graphic design, advertising and promotion, public relations, social media, and video production. LAads: A Marketing Agency handled all these elements for the highly successful 2019 **Before I Die Festival** in Bakersfield, California, a one-day event at Greenlawn Funeral Homes, Cemeteries, and Cremations.

Online Technical Assistance

Your festival will need a web presence. Some festivals have used just a Facebook page as their main conduit of information and online engagement. It's easy to set up a page and use the tools Facebook provides for boosting visibility. Boosting posts requires a budget, part of your advertising costs. A word of caution: Using Facebook, you don't own the online real estate and the page can be taken down by Facebook at any time.

My dedicated festival website, **www.BeforeIDieFestivals.com**, enables people to opt-in to an email list and view videos of past festival sessions. It promotes festival sponsors with links to their websites, has a calendar of upcoming events, and provides background about the festival. My local tech person keeps the website secure while I can still update information and do blog posts.

The first **Before I Die Festival** in Cardiff, Wales, relied on a free Facebook Page to be their online presence. For affordable website designers, check into freelance services through Upwork.com or Fiverr.com.

If you hold festival sessions online, it's good to have a technical person manage that part. You can use a service like Keeper,™ Whova, or other online streaming services, or your favorite IT person. Make sure that you have the rights to post videos of sessions online afterward. You'll want to have your speakers sign a release form giving permission for recording and sharing their talks. A sample video release form is included in Chapter Ten: "Sample Before I Die Festival Materials and Forms."

Promotion

It helps to have a PR-savvy person write and distribute press releases; make interview arrangements on TV, radio, and in local print media; and put out multiple posts on social media channels. These efforts may be handled by more than one person. Since my background is in PR, I did most of the public relations for early festivals. I engaged the services of a freelance PR person for later festivals.

In addition to contacting media individually, you might pay for online news release distribution on services such as EINPresswire.com, eReleases.com, PRNewswire.com, PRWeb.com, Newswire.com, and ExpertClick.com. Links to your festival website in the news releases can help with online visibility.

There are numerous online local event calendars that can list your festival for free and provide more visibility through paid boosting. Sites to look for include your state or local tourism calendars, Allevents.in, CitySpark, Eventbrite, Events.com, Evvnt, HoldMyTicket.com, NextDoor, Patch.com, Yelp for your local market, and online calendar pages for local TV, radio, and print news outlets. Some of these online services provide their calendar of events to local media websites, varying by market.

Video is an important element on social media. You might engage a young person to handle social media and video for your festival. A digital native can make photo posts and enticing short videos to promote the festival before and during the events. Put videos and posts on a page or channel you dedicate to the festival on Facebook, YouTube, TikTok, Twitter, Instagram, Pinterest, and other social media platforms. You can find people to do videos and social media at a reasonable cost through freelance service marketplaces UpWork.com and Fivver.com.

Database Managers

You may want to engage the services of a virtual assistant (VA), employee, or a local volunteer to collect and track information on registrations. As people register, the assistant adds them to an email databank. Use email as well as social media to keep in communication with participants leading up to, during, and after the festival.

You can use your own email system or a marketing service like MailChimp or Constant Contact (many more are out there!) to manage emails. Email marketing platforms offer free and paid versions, depending on the number of emails in your database.

Someone will need to write the emails that get sent to registrants. A virtual assistant who can write effective emails for you may cost more than someone who simply does data entry. You can find virtual assistants and easily engage their services through companies like Upwork.com, Fiverr.com, and other freelancer online sites. Or ask your friends and colleagues who they might recommend!

On-Site Event Managers

As festival coordinator, you can't be in two or more places at once. If you do have multiple events going on, someone needs to be on-site to manage festival details. This person will make official announcements, collect contact information, distribute festival materials, and give credit to the sponsors.

For example, the first **Before I Die Festival** in Albuquerque featured an art show of ceramics that were ideal for holding cremated remains. It was held at an artist's residence, and she was the coordinator of that event. She worked with artist friends to bring a wide range of work together. They promoted the show to their individual lists of contacts. She collected attendee information and distributed festival materials.

During the 2018 **Before I Die New Mexico Festival**, Berardinelli Funeral Home in Santa Fe held a ceramics art show of beautiful urns in their reception center along with a day of festival programming. A funeral director at Berardinelli's coordinated the day's activities in Santa Fe while I managed events in Albuquerque.

The independent Guild Theater in Albuquerque showed movies like *The Seventh Seal*, *Harold and Maude*, and *Defending Your Life* as part of the festival programming. A volunteer at the theater made festival announcements before and after the films and collected prize drawing slips from attendees. Participants provided their contact information for the chance to win prizes from sponsors, such as a free green burial plot, cremation, or urn.

Online Services for Ticketing and Surveys

Even if you don't plan to charge for your festival events, it can be helpful to use a ticketing service to manage registrations and collect information on your attendees. Services such as AllEvents.in, EventBrite, Events.com, Evvnt, HoldMyTicket, and SquadUP offer online calendars that help promote events in your market as well as sell tickets. They will send reminder emails to ticket holders as the event date approaches.

When you set up an account to sell tickets, you link to a bank account with an online processing service such as Square, Stripe, or PayPal to accept monies.

There's no upfront cost to use these services, but they will take a fee from each transaction. The percentage varies by provider.

After the festival is over, it's helpful to ask your attendees what they liked and what could be improved. I've used SurveyMonkey, which offers free and paid options for conducting online surveys. The first festival in the U.K. in 2013 used students at Cardiff University to conduct a follow-up survey of participants. Other online survey services with free and paid options include Google Forms, SurveySparrow, Typeform, Qualtrics, QuestionPro, Alchemer (formerly SurveyGizmo), and Zoho Survey.

Chapter 5

Complementary Business Partners

There are a host of local and national organizations and individuals you can work with to create and promote **Before I Die Festival** events. These businesses and organizations can become sponsors and/or partners, with promotional benefits. Some ideas include:

- **Universities**: As the early festivals in Cardiff, Wales, and Indianapolis, Indiana, illustrated, the support of a university can be immensely helpful. To access those resources, you will need someone who works at the university to be a key person on the festival team.

- **University Continuing Education Programs**: At several **Before I Die New Mexico Festivals**, we worked with the University of New Mexico's Continuing Education program to host a day of symposium presentations at their facility. The university's continuing education program provided the meeting space, tables and chairs, and AV technical assistance. Sponsors had exhibitor tables in the room, and breakfast and lunch were catered. The event was promoted in the UNM Continuing Education catalog for the fall semester and people registered through the program's portal. Osher Lifelong Learning Institutes (OLLI) at 120 universities and colleges throughout the United States can support a festival event.

- **Oasis**: A national organization that serves older adults with lifelong learning opportunities, Oasis can also provide opportunities to hold and promote festival events. Oasis has nine physical Oasis Centers and numerous partner locations that offer in-person and online video courses across the United States.

- **Community Centers**: Jewish community centers (JCCs) and municipal community centers have facilities for meetings, a program person to put on events, and communication channels to members. At the JCC, we held panel discussions with connections to Jewish topics and a demonstration of the Jewish *tahara* ritual of washing and dressing the dead. City-run community centers can also feature programming connected to festival events.

- **Funeral Homes and Cemeteries**: Many funeral homes have reception centers that are perfect for hosting festival events. They can offer behind-the-scenes tours and knowledgeable speakers. Cemeteries can host walking tours that highlight local history and hold other interesting outdoors events.

- **Local Humanities Council Organizations**: In 2021, the New Mexico Humanities Council coordinated the wildly successful Cemetery Stories event, held outdoors in Albuquerque's Historic Fairview Cemetery. They arranged for the stage and chairs, promoted the event, sold tickets, collected money, coordinated the 22 speakers, and provided refreshments and Day of the Dead decorations.

- **Local and Independent Movie Theaters**: Films or documentaries related to death and funerals can be a thought-provoking addition to festival programming. They do set their schedules months in advance, so think ahead. You may have more success working with a local independent movie house rather than a chain-owned theater.

- **Stage Play Theaters**: Stage productions can provide thoughtful additions to the death-and-dying conversation, with conversations after the performance. Some ideas: *Our Town* ends in a cemetery with characters pondering the value of life as we live it. Wit is all about medical treatment and end-of-life. The 2013 **Before I Die Festival** in Cardiff featured *Instinct for Kindness*, a one-man play about assisted death. During the 2020 **Virtual Festival**, we featured several short plays by New Mexico playwright Robert Benjamin, performed online. The plays including *Plots* (about second marriages and final resting places), *Ultimate Precision* (about obituary writing), and *Allocating the Jewels* (about a dying woman finding new homes for her valuables).

- **Shops**: Stores that cater to fans of metaphysical topics or carry Day of the Dead merchandise may help promote or sponsor a festival. In Albuquerque, the Blue Eagle Metaphysical Emporium distributed festival promotional postcards with the free materials they make available to shop patrons. If a shop features the services of psychics or tarot readers, those people might get involved in festival activities. If the facility is large enough, festival events might be held in the store.

- **Local Coroner or Office of the Medical Investigator (OMI)**: Thanks to CSI television shows, people are fascinated by what goes on in the labs of forensic investigators. You may be able to arrange to have the local coroner or OMI conduct an in-person tour as a festival event. If that's not possible, they may provide a speaker from the organization to do a presentation about the actual workings of their office.

- **YMCAs**: A local YMCA may provide space for festival sessions and help promote events to their membership.

- **Estate Planning Attorneys**: A law office can host festival sessions to get potential new clients to literally come in the door.

- **Houses of Worship**: Churches, synagogues, mosques, and other houses of worship have meeting rooms, put together programs for their congregants, and have communication channels about upcoming events. A day of festival programming could be hosted at a large house of worship for the benefit of the congregation as well as the community.

- **Reimagine End of Life**: If you plan to hold an online festival, this nonprofit offers a platform for sharing and promoting your events. Reimagine draws on the arts, design, medicine, and spirituality to transform taboo cultural attitudes around death and grief. Information on registering your event is available at **www.LetsReimagine.org**.

Individuals who could make great additions to festival programming, in alphabetical order, include:

- **Aging in Place Experts**: Many baby boomers, a key demographic for the festival, are interested in staying in their homes as long as possible.

- **Artists**: Ceramic artist contributions were discussed earlier. Those who create *Dia de los Muertos* or death-related art of all kinds can be a great addition to a festival symposium exhibit or other mass gathering. Several festival speaker sessions in Albuquerque were held in the studio of an art center.

- **Authors**: Many authors would be happy to discuss their books related to **Before I Die Festival** topics, such as death, grief, preparing for end-of-life, funeral history, Near Death Experiences (NDEs), the pandemic, pet loss, and much more.

- **Casket Makers**: In New Mexico, we are blessed to have several independent casket makers in the Albuquerque area, as well as Passages International, a major wholesaler of green burial and cremation products. There may be small manufacturers in your area. Consider holding a tour of local casket-making facilities or holding a hands-on workshop for making one's own burial box, cremation container, or urn.

- **Chefs**: Funerals have traditional foods in different cultures. A chef could hold a cooking class for making dishes like funeral potatoes, deviled eggs, and casseroles.

- **Death Doulas**: A relatively new development, these folks, mostly women, are trained to help people prepare for end-of-life. They can be on hand with the dying person as they make their transition. There is much interest in this growing field.

- **Downsizing/Organizing Experts**: Liquidating a household is one of the major changes that death brings. A popular topic for a speaker or panel discussion is how to downsize and still hold on to a family's legacy.

- **Ethics Experts**: Academics or medical personnel who can discuss the challenges of wrestling with end-of-life issues in medical settings without patient guidance may prompt people to prepare their advance medical directives.

- **Genealogy Researchers**: A how-to presentation on exploring the roots of one's family tree can be a session of great interest.

- **Historians**: The history of funerals and embalming, funerals of the famous, strange ways people died, and cemetery tours are all ways to weave history into festival sessions.

- **Hospice Representatives**: A speaker who can discuss hospice care in an engaging way may help people to reap the benefits of hospice services sooner rather than later.

- **Musicians**: The Threshold Choir has groups in over 200 communities around the world. They sing for those at the threshold of life, with songs to die to and grieve to. A concert as a festival event also could be a fundraiser for this worthy cause.

- **Paranormal Investigators/Psychics/NDEs**: In many markets, there are those who investigate "the woo-woo side of death." You can partner with local people who investigate paranormal activities or conduct ghost walks, hold conversations with those who have had Near Death Experiences, and have psychics share their insights. We have held panel discussions with women who communicate with the dead and explored ways to honor and communicate with deceased loved ones.

- **Pet Loss Experts**: Many people cherish their "fur children" and mourn their deaths. Possible speakers include psychologists, veterinarians, and pet cremation service providers.

- **Poets/Storytellers**: A storytelling event or poetry slam about death-related topics can attract younger audiences.

- **Psychologists**: A speaker or panel discussion of psychologists on grief, death avoidance, and related topics can help people better address these issues.

- **Yoga Instructors**: Yoga instructors can hold classes designed to address the physical aspects of grief.

Ask participating speakers to help promote the festival to their social media channels and their email lists. Have them send people to your festival website to register. These festival partners can also provide ideas for interesting session topics, which we will cover in detail in the next chapter.

Chapter 6

Before I Die Festival Topics

What topics and activities could you feature during your **Before I Die Festival**? The field is wide open! Lectures, Death Cafes, panel discussions, field trips, the performing arts, behind-the-scenes tours, games, and outside-the-box activities are all great options. Do what works for you!

Here are ideas for fascinating sessions, including ideas from attendees on what they wanted to see at future festivals.

Session Topics

- **Aging in Place**: How to safely stay in one's home is a topic of interest to baby boomers and seniors.

- **The Arts and Death**: Performing arts, including music, poetry, storytelling, and dance, in addition to artwork and theater, can be a great way to start conversations.

- **Autopsies and the OMI**: Tour a coroner's office or Office of the Medical Investigator, or have a speaker talk about the real-world workings of forensic investigations and autopsies.

- **Celebrants on Creating Ceremonies**: Certified funeral celebrants could discuss the aspects that make for a healing, satisfying memorial service, with or without religious involvement.

- **Cemetery History**: Invite speakers who are taphophiles, cemetery enthusiasts who can speak about the history of cemetery burials, headstone symbols, and related topics. This presentation can be virtual or an on-site visit to a cemetery.

- **Cremation**: Explain the cremation process in detail, tour a crematorium, show unprocessed remains in the retort, discuss options for final placement or dispersal, and related legalities.

- **Death Cafe Discussions**: The Death Cafe movement offers an opportunity to talk about mortality issues in an open and supportive environment. The ground rules for holding a Death Cafe are included in the **Before I Die Festival in a Box** or available to download from **www.DeathCafe.com**.

- **Death and Digital Assets**: What happens to your social media and other online accounts after you die? An expert can discuss ways people can be prepared to shut down others' online lives.

- **Death Doulas**: A panel of death doulas can describe what they do and how they can help the dying and their families plan for the inevitable.

- **Dealing with Dementia and Death**: This tough topic can best be discussed with those who have cared for or are caring for a loved one with dementia.

- **Documentary Films**: Many fascinating documentaries illuminate issues such as medical aid-in-dying, funeral rituals, addressing mortality, and more. A listing of documentaries is included in Chapter Eight, "Mortality Movies and TV Shows."

- **Donating a Body to Science**: Speakers from donation organizations can discuss topics such as the differences between organ and tissue donation and whole-body donation, getting a free cremation, and conditions that prevent a donation.

- **Downsizing and Dealing with Loved Ones' Possessions**: What do you do with all that stuff? Experts can address what to keep, what to let go of, and how to approach what can be a huge project.

- **Estate Planning**: An estate attorney can provide an overview of legal aspects of wills, trusts, advance medical directives, and how to pass along one's valuables to those you wish to inherit them.

- **Financial Planning**: Have a financial expert talk about how to avoid outliving your financial resources and saving/investing so you can retire.

- **Funeral Director Panel Discussion**: Bring together funeral directors from several funeral homes to have an open discussion about what people should know before there's a death in the family.

- **Funerals in Different Cultures and Religions**: This topic ideally would be presented by individuals who represent these different cultures and religions.

- **Funeral History**: Have a historian talk about different aspects of death rituals, such as Egyptian mummification, Victorian funeral objects, rituals in different cultures, U.S. Presidential funerals, and the evolution of embalming.

- **Genealogy Research**: Learn how to trace your family tree with tips and tools shared by an experienced researcher.

- **Green Burial/New Trends in Death Care**: At the 2020 **Virtual Festival**, an online panel of cemeterians from across the country discussed new approaches to cemetery use and creative community outreach. Green burial is of great interest.

- **Grief Topics**: Have an expert on grief, or a panel, discuss different types of grief and how to address them. Some yoga teachers specialize in classes that address the physical impacts of grief.

- **Hospice and Palliative Care**: The difference between hospice and palliative care is not widely understood. You could have a discussion panel with hospice representatives and medical professionals who can spell out the benefits of these services for improving end-of-life experiences.

- **Medical Aid in Dying (MAID)**: As of late 2022, 10 U.S. states, the District of Columbia, and all Canadian provinces allow terminally ill patients to take medication to avoid excess suffering and control the timing of their deaths. Another 13 states have legislation pending.

Consider holding a session to discuss the use of MAID or potential for legalization in your state. Related topics include voluntary stopping of eating and drinking and other ways to achieve a peaceful death. Organizations such as Compassion & Choices and Final Exit Network can direct you to qualified speakers on these topics.

- **Medical Documents**: There's plenty to learn about appointing a medical advocate or healthcare Power of Attorney (POA), preparing advance medical directives, and documents such as the Five Wishes form, MOLST or POLST forms, and living wills.

- **Obituary and Eulogy Writing**: This could be a session with a speaker and/or a hands-on workshop. Participants could be invited to share what they've written.

- **Pandemic Funeral Impacts**: Funeral directors can update the public on the impact of pandemics current and past on funeral service.

- **Pet Loss**: Pet loss is often a cause for disenfranchised grief; a panel about pet loss could include a pet loss psychotherapist, a veterinarian, and a representative of a funeral home that has pet services.

- **The Process of Dying**: Have an experienced speaker explain what to look for as death approaches. Good candidates are hospice or palliative care nurses or death doulas. Some have written books on the topic.

- **The Woo-Woo Side of Death**: There is a range of topics that could be explored and activities that could be held – after-death communications, Near Death Experiences, paranormal investigations, psychics, and writing letters to the deceased.

Other Activities

Here are additional events that various **Before I Die Festivals** have held in the U.K. and the U.S. These other activities could be run by partner organizations under the umbrella of a local **Before I Die Festival**.

- **Art Shows**: These could be held in cafes, galleries, artist studios, or other locations.
- **Before I Die Wall**: The Before I Die Wall concept, featured in a TED talk by Candy Chang in 2012, has spread around the world. A giant

chalkboard with the words "Before I Die I Want To…" provides an opportunity for people to publicly declare what they'd like to do before they die. These walls can be set up in various public settings. More information on how to create a Before I Die Wall is available at **www.BeforeIDieProject.com**.

- **Behind-the-Scenes Tours**: Funeral homes, crematoria, cemeteries, and coroners can take people on guided tours of their operations. People are fascinated with the workings of these places.

- **Book Discussions**: The authors of books related to end-of-life issues could speak and discuss these topics with audiences at local bookstores, cafes, or wherever you hold most of your festival events.

- **Cemetery Visits**: Hold a "headstone hunt" competition to find specific memorial markers for notable or interesting individuals. Tour a local green burial ground or historic cemetery with an informed tour guide. A cemetery could also set up a themed tour such as "Murder and Mayhem" or "Love and Death" stories.

- **Day of the Dead/*Dia de los Muertos* Festival**: Hold a community event with music, art, food, dancing, costumes, and makeup, a parade, and hands-on activities celebrating this death positive holiday that originated in Central America and Mexico. November 1 and 2 are the dates for *Dia de los Muertos*. The event can be held on the weekend closest to Halloween.

- **Millennial Morticians Panel**: In New Mexico, "Millennial Morticians with ABQ Brews" was held at a local craft brew pub. The panel discussion is a great opportunity for young people in the funeral/cemetery business to share their experiences. The audience included the public as well as other young professionals in the field. Come up with your own local twist on the title for a Millennial Morticians panel.

- **Mortuary Mall**: Funeral homes and cemeteries can display their products outdoors as weather permits. At past festivals, products such as vaults, memorial markers, urns, caskets, and cremation jewelry have been featured. Attendees can view and touch products and ask questions of knowledgeable staff.

- **Movies**: In addition to documentaries on end-of-life issues, consider showing feature films that involve funerals, death discussions, the afterlife, or related topics. These can be hosted in a movie theater, funeral home, or other locations. For a list of suggested films, documentaries, and TV shows, see Chapter Eight: "Mortality Movies and TV Shows."

- **Newly-Dead® Bingo**: Hold a Bingo game session featuring cards that highlight end-of-life and funeral planning topics as the squares to match. The emcee can share interesting bits of information as the game progresses. Game cards are available from Gail Rubin (see Chapter Eleven: "More from Gail Rubin") and included in the **Before I Die Festival in a Box**.

- **Newly-Dead® The Game**: Like the old TV game show, *The Newlywed Game*, this activity quizzes couples on how well they know each other – but it's all about how well they know each other's last wishes. There's also a Singles Edition, which can be used to allow all audience members to play along. The game is included in the **Before I Die Festival in a Box**.

- **Obon Festival Observation**: Japan's Obon Festival, a time to honor ancestors and deceased loved ones, usually takes place in August. It provides a cultural teaching opportunity related to death rituals and observances.

- **Party with a Purpose**: Parties offer an opportunity to showcase reception centers at funeral homes and cemeteries. You can celebrate life while honoring the fact that we all have a 100% mortality rate.

- **Visit the Coroner's Office or OMI**: People are fascinated with behind-the-scenes tours at these offices, if the local authorities allow visits.

- **Visit a Local Casket Maker's Workshop**: If you have a local craftsperson who makes caskets, this can be a great learning and marketing opportunity for everyone involved.

Workshop Ideas

Hands-on workshops are engaging and memorable, and participants can go home with the fruits of their labor, to continue their work and potentially start and invite conversations with other family members.

- Obituary writing for yourself or others

- Build an *ofrenda* or home altar (a collection of objects honoring deceased loved ones), making paper marigolds, decorating picture frames
- Memorialization activities honoring deceased children, adults, and pets
- Preparing your advance healthcare directives, POLST or MOLST forms, and Five Wishes form
- Write an Upon My Death letter (the Bare Bones checklist to write such a letter is included in Chapter Ten: "Sample Promotional and News Materials")
- Demonstrate the Jewish and Muslim *tahara* ritual of washing and dressing the dead, using a mannequin or live volunteer to be the body
- Building a casket or decorating a cremation container
- Making your own death mask or ritual mandala
- Putting the "Fun" in Funeral Planning: Funerals are the parties no one wants to plan. However, with enough mental distance from death, it can be a creative experience to plan one's own life celebration.

The possibilities are wide-ranging and upbeat. Your festival needs to entertain while educating about the inevitability of death.

Chapter 7

Before I Die Festival Event Logistics

In this chapter, we'll explore festival logistics. Logistics is the detailed coordination of a complex operation involving many people, facilities, and/or supplies. There are many moving parts to a **Before I Die Festival**, and here's where you'll get a sense of how to pull it all together.

We will cover how to secure locations and speakers; how to video record sessions and share them online; ways to collect information about your festival attendees; more information about Before I Die walls; ideas for funeral homes and cemeteries to hold a Mortuary Mall and behind-the-scenes tours; and post-event evaluation.

Securing Event Locations

Ideally, allow six months or more to plan out your festival. You might plan to hold events tied to certain days devoted to end-of-life issues. For example, April 16 is National Health Care Decisions Day, to inspire, educate, and empower the public and providers about the importance of advance care planning. Since it's right after Tax Day, you can employ the theme of Death and Taxes!

October 30 is Create a Great Funeral Day, devoted to planning your own funeral. The day was registered with Chase's Calendar of Events by Stephanie

West Allen in 1999. It gives people an easy excuse to start the conversation about funeral plans.

The Halloween/Day of the Dead/Celtic Samhain connection in late October/early November is a popular time for a **Before I Die Festival**. April 4 or 5 is Qingming, a Chinese festival also called Tomb Sweeping Day. The Japanese Obon festival takes place in mid- to late August, when deceased ancestors are welcomed for a visit.

With your target dates in mind, look for venues. As you secure sponsors, working with local funeral homes or cemeteries can build in a place to hold events at their reception centers. Theaters could host films and live plays. Community centers, JCCs, YMCAs, continuing education centers at local universities, and Oasis programs can offer places to hold events as part of their programming.

If you plan to offer a hybrid in-person/online option, make sure the technology is available. This includes high-speed internet access, wi-fi services, and large-screen TVs or projection screens on site. You also want access to a laptop computer with external microphone and camera to get the best audiovisual input.

Arranging for Speakers

Once you've identified the time frame and locations for your festival, you can start approaching speakers. Begin with local people. There is likely a treasure trove of great speakers you can discover right in your own back yard.

Your sponsors can provide speakers. Speaking opportunities can be one benefit of sponsorship, depending on the investment level. It makes great sense to have sessions with estate planning attorneys, financial planners, funeral directors, and professionals in cremation, hospice, downsizing, and other fields. Speakers can be from national or local sponsor organizations.

Schedule a variety of topics and speakers over the course of the day to keep participants engaged. A wide variety of topics in one day could include a session on funeral history, an in-person Death Cafe, a session on obituary writing, a session on organ/body donation, and a behind-the-scenes tour of a crematorium.

Online Speaker Resources

Online presentations in a hybrid setting can provide speakers from almost anywhere. These people have graciously expressed their willingness to speak at **Before I Die Festivals**. Some may ask for a fee. Here are their names, contact information, and topics they can cover.

- **Garrick Colwell, Kitchen Table Conversations**. Garrick is a hospice volunteer (since 1987), a Certified Grief Recovery Specialist, a Certified Grief Educator, and a Respecting Choices Advance Care Planning Instructor. He and his late wife, Kinsloe, co-created Kitchen Table Conversations, a nonprofit that empowers people to have conversations about end-of-life issues, advance care planning, and grief education. He is based in Texas. PH: 512-787-3402 | Email: **Garrick@KitchenTableConversations.org** | **www.KitchenTableConversations.org**.

- **Matthew Van Drimmelen, Full-Circle Aftercare**. Matt is an expert on assisting families with the complexities of settling personal and estate matters after a death. He can help the bereaved understand the many challenges they face and how to manage them. He is based in Utah. Contact him by email: **matt@full-circlecare.com** | **www.Full-CircleCare.com**.

- **Coleen Ellis, CT, CPLC, Two Hearts Pet Loss Center**. Coleen is a pioneer in helping humans cope with pet loss and a dynamic speaker. She is based in Texas. PH: 317-966-0096 | Email: **coleen@twoheartspetlosscenter.com** | **www.TwoHeartsPetLossCenter.com**.

- **Heather Leigh, Grief Recovery Specialist, Certified Funeral Celebrant, and General Manager of Greenhaven Memorial Gardens**. Heather can speak on a range of topics including the grief process, pet loss, new trends in memorial services, and green burial. She is based in South Carolina. PH: 803-419-7110 | Email: **Heather@greenhavenmemorialgardens.com** | **www.GreenhavenMemorialGardens.com**.

- **Allen Klein, MA, CSP, Award-Winning Professional Speaker, Best-Selling Author, TEDx presenter**. Klein's wife died at the age of 34. Her sense of humor showed him how powerful this therapeutic tool can be, even during loss. Through his presentations and his books (i.e., *Embracing Life After Loss*), Klein shows people how to find humor in their not-so-funny stuff. He is based in San Francisco. Email: **allen@allenklein.com** | **www.AllenKlein.com**.

- **Martie McNabb, Founder, Thingtide Show & Tale® LLC**. Martie is a personal historian/legacy artist and creator of Show & Tale story-sharing gatherings. While the best things in life aren't things, they hold the best life stories. At these highly interactive in-person or virtual gatherings, people are invited to bring a treasured object or photo and share its story. PH: 718-398-1519 | Email: **info@showandtales.com** | **www.ShowandTales.com**.

- **Petra Orloff, Beloved**. Petra writes compelling obituaries and eulogies and can speak to participants about how to craft these important documents. She is based in Michigan. PH: 248-894-7076 | Email: **Petra@beloved-press.com** | **www.Beloved-Press.com**.

- **Anne Moss Rogers, Mental Health and Suicide Prevention Motivational Speaker, Author and Trainer**. Anne Moss' son died by suicide, and now she helps people to recognize warning signs and understand this unique grief process. She is based in Richmond, Virginia. You can contact her through her websites, **www.AnneMossRogers.com** and **www.EmotionallyNaked.com**, or through this form: **https://annemoss.com/contact-2/**.

- **Gail Rubin, CT, The Doyenne of Death**.® Gail is a pioneering death educator who uses humor, film clips, and outside-the-box activities to encourage planning for end-of-life issues. She held the first Death Cafe in the United States west of the Mississippi, created **Newly-Dead® The Game** and has hosted multiple **Before I Die Festivals**. She is based in New Mexico. PH: 505-265-7215 | Email: **Gail@agoodgoodbye.com**.

- **Kyle Tevlin, Founder, I Want a Fun Funeral**. Kyle offers talks and upbeat workshops on planning your own goodbye party and creating celebrations that make a positive difference in the world. She is based in Pennsylvania. PH: 215-348-4306 | Email: **Kyle@IWantAFunFuneral.com** | **www.IWantAFunFuneral.com**.

Additions and changes to this list can be found online at the Speakers Page at **www.BeforeIDieFestivals.com**.

Festival Video Recordings

Recording video of festival sessions offers you several benefits. The information shared on any given topic will be valuable for others to hear after the festival is over. An enduring video on YouTube with credit and links to festival sponsors is a marketing benefit to offer in your sponsorship proposal. Videos can be posted to your festival website, extending public interest in the next festival.

Make sure to get a speaker release agreement signed before the event starts. This helps cover the you as the event organizer from legal challenges that may arise after the festival. The release states that the speaker is okay with your using their video, voice, and images without further compensation. Some speakers will not be okay with putting their video online or may only agree to posting it for a limited period. Honor their wishes. Most speakers welcome the additional exposure provided by an online video. A sample agreement is included in the appendix of forms. Please consult with your own attorney for legal advice on this matter.

Also make sure the audience knows that festival sessions are being recorded. Make an announcement at the start of each session along the lines of "This festival session is being recorded for sharing online afterwards. Your continued presence at this session implies your agreement to being a part of the recording." If any audience members are uncomfortable about appearing in such videos, you can designate a section of the room where they will not be viewable on camera. Or, put a mark on someone's name badge to indicate they do not want to be seen in any video recording.

Collecting Attendee Information

You need to collect information on festival attendees for several reasons:
- You need to communicate with attendees before, during, and after the festival, to keep participants engaged, excited, and informed about last-minute changes.
- The contact information for attendees is a benefit that can be offered to sponsors. You can determine the best communications channels for future events by asking how they found out about the festival.
- If a funeral home or cemetery is hosting the festival, these contacts are the warm leads generated by the investment of time and money in the event.

There are several ways to collect this information:
- Offer online registration, using an event management program like Whova, Google forms, or a shopping cart program (do an internet search for "shopping cart software" for the latest recommendations), or use a ticketing service like EventBrite.
- Entice them to complete on-site prize drawing slips of paper in exchange for the chance to win valuable gifts (see sample form in Chapter Ten).

- While you would already have participants' information to ask for post-event survey feedback, you might also share the survey on your festival's social media channels for additional reach and connections.

To show you how a funeral home or cemetery can benefit from collecting information from attendees, consider the 2019 **Before I Die Festival** held in Bakersfield, California, by Greenlawn Funeral Homes, Cemeteries, and Cremations. Their one-day event drew 200 attendees from a wide range of ages and ethnicities. They collected 113 prize drawing entries to win significant funeral-related prizes, such as a cremation niche for two and ground burial for two. In just the first two days of follow-up after the festival, the preneed sales staff closed over $80,000 in sales. In additional follow-up, they sold 20 preneed packages. This was a stellar return on investment for the company.

Mortuary Malls and Behind-the-Scenes Tours

What is a Mortuary Mall? Most funeral homes have a selection room where customers can look at urns, a few caskets (depending on available floor space), keepsakes, and scaled down examples of vaults. A Mortuary Mall is an outdoor display where full-size vaults, monuments, memorial markers, and caskets can be displayed and discussed. Local and national providers of caskets and urns, artists and jewelers, monument makers, and other funeral product providers can show and talk about their wares. A tour of a funeral home's selection room can serve as a mini–Mortuary Mall.

A Mortuary Mall also makes a great visual for local TV news coverage. At Greenlawn's **Before I Die Festival** in Bakersfield, they employed the shade structures used for graveside funerals for Mortuary Mall shade in the parking lot in front of the funeral home. Their casket supplier was on hand to answer people's questions. They displayed burial vaults, cremation jewelry, and samples of memorial markers created on-site. Reporters shot video of the Mortuary Mall and tagged along on the behind-the-scenes tours of the preparation room and crematory.

Holding behind-the-scenes tours as part of a **Before I Die Festival** can help answer the questions people have about what happens in funeral homes, crematories, and cemeteries.

French Funerals & Cremations in Albuquerque hosted a day of festival events at their cemetery, Sunset Memorial Park. The cemetery has a building on-site where several panel discussions and a Death Cafe were held. A Mortuary Mall took place outdoors in the shade of their pavilion next to the Centennial

Cremation Garden. Displays included kosher caskets from local provider Fathers Building Futures, eco-friendly caskets and urns from Albuquerque-based national distributor Passages International, and samples of processed cremated remains from Parting Stone, a Santa Fe-based company.

For a behind-the-scenes experience, the cemetery manager spoke about the cremation process to an audience in the Chester T. French Memorial Chapel, part of the cemetery's mausoleum. The chapel has a cremation retort adjacent to the ceremonial space that allows attendees to witness the start of a cremation.

More than 30 people attended a talk about the cremation process. Following the talk, the door to the room with the retort was opened. With permission from the decedent's representative, the bones from a human body that had been cremated but not yet processed were shown to the session attendees. The speaker did caution audience members if they were uncomfortable about viewing cremated remains to avoid this part of the tour. Most attendees crowded around the door of the retort, interested, engaged, and inquisitive.

With the rise in percentage of people choosing cremation as a disposition method, this will continue to be a topic of burning interest. A growing number of states allow other disposition methods, such as alkaline hydrolysis (water-based cremation) and Natural Organic Reduction (NOR), also known as body composting. A funeral home that utilizes these alternative approaches can spontaneously market these services by holding a behind-the-scenes tour that highlights these eco-friendly disposition methods.

Death Cafes

Death Cafes are a great element to include in a **Before I Die Festival**. Opportunities to openly discuss the many aspects of death and dying are few. With a skilled facilitator, Death Cafes can provide a satisfying conversation for festival participants. Depending on your schedule, you could hold a single Death Cafe or host one each day of a multi-day event.

A funeral home with a reception room or a cemetery with an event center is an ideal place to hold a festival Death Cafe. Groups of fewer than twenty audience members can hold one conversation. For more than 20, you may wish to break the conversation into smaller groupings and seat them at round tables. The food and drink can be catered or provided by volunteers.

To call your gathering a Death Cafe, you need to follow certain rules:
- No agenda, no guest speakers, no leading participants to any conclusion, product, or course of action – participants lead the discussion with a facilitator

- Provide an open, respectful, and confidential space where people can safely express their views
- Hold the event on a not-for-profit basis, although donations are allowed
- Stress that this is not a bereavement support group or grief counseling session
- Offer refreshing and nourishing food and drink – and cake!

A sample overview of the ground rules for holding a Death Cafe is included in Chapter Ten: "Sample Before I Die Festival Materials and Forms."

You can also download the complete set of ground rules as a PDF from **www.DeathCafe.com/how**.

If you don't want to follow these Death Cafe rules (such as having a guest speaker), you can still have a death discussion gathering. Just call it something else. Some clever options you can use include Death and Donuts, Coffee and Coffins, Cupcakes and Caskets, Death Discussions, and Mortality and Munchies.

If you want to include a film showing before a group discussion, call it something like Talking Mortality at the Movies, Movie Night at the Funeral Home, or Funeral Film Conversations.

Before I Die Walls

Before I Die Walls started as an art project in New Orleans. Candy Chang wanted to honor the death of a dear friend by turning an abandoned house into the first Before I Die Wall. She painted the plywood that covered the building with chalkboard paint. Using a homemade stencil, she inscribed multiple lines of the words, "Before I die I want to _____." People immediately began using the chalk she provided to answer that question. The wall became an icebreaker for meaningful conversations on death and emotional health.

Her 2012 TED Talk about the project launched Before I Die, a global art project that invites people to reflect upon their mortality and consider what matters most to them. According to the Before I Die Project, more than 5,000 Before I Die Walls have been created in over 78 countries and more than 36 languages.

A Before I Die Wall can be used in a **Before I Die Festival** to draw attention to festival events, supplement the activities at a festival location, and become a public year-round reminder to make the most of each day.

While most Before I Die Walls are attached to buildings or structures, they can be portable. In Albuquerque, French Funerals & Cremations created movable Before I Die Walls. They used sturdy steel plates connected at angles as the chalkboard. The plates were about eight feet tall, with "Before I Die" on magnetic stickers at the top and a cup for chalk at waist level. The way the panels were connected created a stable, freestanding structure for participants to write upon.

The plates were taken to public events where the funeral home had a booth to generate leads. During the New Mexico **Before I Die Festival**, their walls were set up on the campus of a local community college and during a TEDxABQ talk event. Much of the year, the walls stood at the Pavilion in their cemetery, Sunset Memorial Park. People of all ages would write their thoughts upon these walls. When the chalk filled the space, they would wipe the walls clean for others to share their thoughts.

You can find the resources and a step-by-step guide on how to build and install a Before I Die Wall at **www.BeforeIDieProject.com**.

Post-Event Evaluation and Report

When the event is over, it's helpful to write a report to sponsors and partners summarizing festival specifics: event dates; number of attendees; the best attended events; how the festival was publicized; news coverage; festival sponsors; whether the event made money, broke even, or lost money; and data from a follow-up survey of attendees. Sponsors should get this report as part of their support. The report also serves as a great basis to guide future festival undertakings.

You can use a survey service or create a Google forms survey to collect feedback from festival attendees. Questions to ask include the following:
- How many sessions did you attend?
- How old are you?
- Are you male, female, other, or prefer not to say?
- Do you prefer in-person, online, or hybrid events?
- What was your favorite event at the festival?
- What other topics would you like to see addressed?
- How did you find out about the festival? (Methods could include, for instance, social media, email, postcard, newspaper coverage, TV coverage, radio interview, word of mouth, advertisements in specific outlets, and billboards.)
- What is your preferred time of year to hold the festival?
- What are your preferred communication channels (email, mail, phone, social media, other)?
- What did you like best about the festival?

This feedback can help guide improvements for future festivals.

Chapter 8

Mortality Movies and TV Shows

Movie Night at a funeral home or cemetery can be a great conversation starter. After viewing a film or selected TV show episodes, you can have experts facilitate conversation with the audience.

This chapter offers suggestions for **Before I Die Festival** movies, documentaries, and TV show episodes, with short descriptions and the topics they raise for discussion after viewing. Always watch a video before scheduling it for a festival. You want to know exactly what the video contains, including rough language, sexual references or scenes, and sensitive topics such as drug use and suicide. Should it raise issues for your community's sensibilities, find a different video to show.

To legally show films and TV shows outside of a movie theater, you need an umbrella license from the Motion Picture Licensing Corporation (**www.MPLC.org**). As part of the arrangement, it is forbidden to charge people to watch the film. If you are working with a movie theater to show festival films, they already have the needed permits to charge people.

Films Featuring Funerals and Funeral Directors

Bernie (2011 – PG-13, 1 hr. 44 min.) In this comedy based on a true crime story, affable mortician Bernie Tiede strikes up a friendship with wealthy widow Marjorie Nugent… until things go tragically wrong. Provides insights into elements of the funeral business and the many roles funeral directors play; and is a great conversation starter. Stars Jack Black, Shirley MacLaine, and Matthew McConaughey.

Death at a Funeral (2007 – R, 1 hr. 30 min.) In this comedy, chaos ensues when a man tries to expose a dark secret regarding a recently deceased patriarch of a dysfunctional British family. Shows a funeral at home, the challenge of paying for a funeral and preparing a eulogy, and the general stress a death in the family can cause. An American version of this film, made in 2010, features an African-American family, starring Chris Rock and Martin Lawrence. Peter Dinklage is in both versions of the film.

Departures (2008 – PG-13, 2 hr. 10 min.) This charming Oscar-winning Japanese film follows the journey of an unemployed cellist who takes a job preparing the dead for funerals. Shows the importance of encountering the dead, Japanese traditions for funerals and cremation, and how grief can be repressed and expressed. Dialogue is in Japanese with English subtitles.

Elizabethtown (2005 – PG-13, 2 hr. 3 min.) This romantic comedy with a wonderful soundtrack incorporates the similarities of weddings and funerals; the clash of cultures between people in the South and the West regarding burial and cremation; a creative memorial service; and an ash-scattering road trip. Stars include Orlando Bloom, Kirsten Dunst, and Susan Sarandon.

Eulogy (2004 – R, 1 hr. 31 min.) This black comedy follows three generations of a family as they come together for the funeral of the patriarch, unveiling a host of family secrets. Shows a variation of a Viking funeral, the reading of the will, and the challenge of saying the right words at a funeral. Includes a scene with cannabis smoking. Stars Ray Romano and Hank Azaria.

Get Low (2009 – PG-13, 1hr. 43 min.) This film is based on a true story of a man who threw his own funeral party while he was still alive. Set in the 1930s, it provides a glimpse into the evolution of the funeral business and shows the elements of planning and implementing an unorthodox funeral. Stars Robert Duvall, Bill Murray, and Sissy Spacek.

Grand Theft Parsons (2003 – PG-13, 1hr. 28 min.) This film is based on the true story of the hijacking of musician Gram Parsons' body after his untimely death in 1973 from an overdose at the age of 26. His road manager, Phil Kaufman, steals the body to fulfill a pledge to set his spirit free in Joshua Tree National Park. Includes insights on body shipment, wills, hearses, and setting a body on fire in the desert. Stars Johnny Knoxville, Robert Forster, and Christina Applegate.

Harold and Maude (1971 – PG-13, 1 hr. 31 min.) This cult classic features Harold, a rich young man who is obsessed with death, who meets lively septuagenarian Maude at a funeral. Shows several funerals, an iconic Jaguar hearse, and provides food for thought on living life to the fullest and exiting on one's own terms. Stars Ruth Gordon and Bud Cort and features a great soundtrack by Cat Stevens.

Just Buried (2007 – PG-13, 1 hr. 34 min.) A young man inherits a nearly bankrupt funeral home from his estranged father and falls in love with the female mortician on staff. It's a quirky comedy that explains embalming in detail, shows how pacemakers can make a crematorium explode, and looks at other elements of running a funeral home.

The Loved One (1965 – unrated, 2 hr. 2 min.) This satire of the funeral business skewers casket sales, funeral services, pet deaths and cemeteries, embalming, and more. Stars Robert Morse as a young British poet who plans a funeral for his uncle (who died by suicide) and goes to work at a Hollywood cemetery/funeral home/pet funeral service. Liberace appears as an outrageous casket salesman.

My Girl (1991 – PG, 1 hr. 42 min.) A sweet story about a young girl growing up in a family-owned funeral home. Her mother died giving birth to her, and her funeral director father contends with balancing work and home life. Shows funeral home operations in the 1970s, that funeral directors have lives beyond their work, and different aspects of grief. Stars Anna Chlumsky, Macaulay Culkin, Dan Aykroyd, and Jamie Lee Curtis.

My Mexican Shivah (2007 – not rated, 1 hr. 38 min.) This comedy from Mexico focuses on Jewish funeral traditions, including the rituals leading up to the funeral through the seven-day mourning period after the burial. Dialogue is in Spanish and Yiddish with English subtitles.

Nora's Will (2008 – not rated, 1 hr. 32 min.) This award-winning comedy/drama from Mexico focuses on Jewish funeral traditions related to suicide, keeping the deceased company prior to burial, scheduling around holidays, and more. Dialogue is Spanish with English subtitles.

The Six Wives of Henry Lefay (2009 – PG-13, 1hr. 35 min.) A comedic cautionary tale for those who don't make funeral plans or those who make plans and don't keep up with life's changes. Henry Lefay's daughter tries to arrange her father's funeral while contending with his multiple ex-wives. Stars include Tim Allen, Elisha Cuthbert, and Andie MacDowell.

Undertaking Betty (2002 – PG-13, 1 hr. 34 min.) Originally titled Plots with a View, this comedy focuses on a woman whose husband is cheating on her and a traditional undertaker who has been in love with her since childhood. A progressive funeral director, new to this small town in Wales, shakes things up with personalized celebrations of life, including a Star Trek funeral, and new marketing ideas. Stars Brenda Blethyn, Alfred Molina, and Christopher Walken.

TV Shows about Funerals

Want to use a video to teach and engage people to discuss death and funerals in under an hour? Try these TV show episodes for great conversation-starting content. Many are available through streaming services.

The Mary Tyler Moore Show – "Chuckles Bites the Dust" 1975 (Season 6, Episode 7, 30 minutes) Mary thinks the death of Chuckles the Clown is nothing to laugh about – until the funeral. TV Guide rated this the greatest TV episode of all time. While death is the primary topic, it's very funny and thoughtful, opening the door to funeral planning conversations.

All in the Family – "Stretch Cunningham, Goodbye" 1977 (Season 7, Episode 19, 30 minutes) Archie Bunker prepares a eulogy for a work colleague and faces a surprise at the funeral. This episode can start a conversation about funerals, eulogy writing, and how much we truly know about the people in our lives.

Six Feet Under – This Emmy Award-winning series, which originally ran on HBO from 2001 to 2005, focuses on the family-operated Fisher Funeral Home in Los Angeles. Every 60-minute episode starts with a death, and follows with the funeral arrangements and memorial event. It was produced with input from actual funeral directors and details real trends in the industry.

While just about any episode would be a conversation starter, be aware that, as an HBO series, curse words are abundant in the dialogue and sexual scenes may be too risqué for a **Before I Die Festival** audience.

My top episode picks are the pilot episode, when Nate Fisher Sr. is killed in an accident and the family comes together to decide the fate of the funeral home; "It's the Most Wonderful Time of the Year" (Season 2, Episode 8) featuring a biker funeral and the death anniversary of Nate Sr.; and "All Alone" (Season 5, Episode 10) which features the first green burial shown on television.

The Kominsky Method – This award-winning Netflix drama/comedy series from 2018 to 2021 focuses on an aging acting coach, played by Michael Douglas, as he contends with illness, death, and, eventually, estate issues. "An Agent Grieves" (Season 1, Episode 2) shows how a letter of instruction can help a grieving family plan the perfect over-the-top funeral. Be aware the series uses many curse words, so review an episode before deciding to use this program.

Movies about Medical Treatment and End-of-Life Issues

50/50 (2010 – R, 1hr. 40 min.) Inspired by a true story, this comedy centers on a 27-year-old who learns of his rare cancer diagnosis, and his subsequent struggle to beat the disease. Illustrates the difficulty of communicating about serious medical diagnoses. Stars Joseph Gordon-Levitt, with Seth Rogan as his best friend who tries to be helpful.

Blackbird (2019 – R, 1 hr. 37 min.) Susan Sarandon stars as a terminally ill mother who brings her family together one last time before she chooses medical aid in dying. Examines issues related to death with dignity, life with meaning, family dynamics, and saying goodbye.

Checking Out (2005 – PG-13, 1 hr. 34 min.) Peter Falk is Morris Applebaum, a 90-year-old stage actor. He's decided he's lived long enough and plans to die by suicide after gathering the family for his big birthday. This comedy can prompt conversations about medical aid-in-dying and related issues.

Critical Care (1997 – R, 1hr. 47 min.) James Spader stars as a hospital resident put in the middle of a legal battle between two half-sisters over whether to pull their comatose dad's life support. Sidney Lumet directed this scathing comedy about medical care, insurance, and difficult decisions in the ICU.

The Descendants (2011 – R, 1 hr. 55 min.) George Clooney plays a husband whose wife is on life support. He wrestles with issues of keeping her alive and the challenge of connecting with his two daughters. Shows the importance of advance medical directives, doctor-patient communications, and helping family and friends cope with a serious medical situation.

The Doctor (1991 – PG-13, 2 hr. 2 min.) William Hurt stars as a self-centered heart surgeon who is diagnosed with throat cancer. As a patient, he becomes better able to empathize with his patients and appreciate life outside his career.

The End (1978 – R, 1 hr. 40 min.) A slapstick comedy with Burt Reynolds playing a man told by a doctor he doesn't have much longer to live. He makes multiple failed attempts at suicide and ponders life and death. Also stars Sally Field and Dom DeLuise.

The Savages (2007 – R, 1 hr. 53 min.) Laura Linney and Philip Seymour Hoffman play adult children estranged for 20 years from their abusive father, who has developed dementia. They struggle to discuss his medical care, advance health directives, and funeral plans in this comedy-drama.

The Shootist (1976 – PG, 1 hr. 40 min.) John Wayne copes with cancer in his last film, both as his character J.B. Books and in real life. He plays a gunfighter looking to spend his last days with a minimum of pain and a maximum of dignity. Shows funeral planning and the state of cancer care in 1901. Also stars Lauren Bacall and Ron Howard.

Still Alice (2014 – PG-13, 1 hr. 41 min.) Alice Howland is a linguistics professor whose family bonds are tested when she is diagnosed with early onset Alzheimer's disease. This film offers a powerful introduction to discussions of dementia. Julianne Moore won the best actress Oscar for this film, also starring Alec Baldwin and Kristen Stewart.

Two Weeks (2006 – R, 1 hr. 42 min.) Sally Field stars in this bittersweet comedy as a mother dying of ovarian cancer. Her four adult children gather at her house. Highlights details of hospice care, funeral planning, family dynamics, and passing along heirlooms.

Wit (2001 – PG-13, 1 hr. 39 min.) Based on the Pulitzer Prize-winning play directed by Mike Nichols. Emma Thompson is a cancer patient in experimental treatment for stage four ovarian cancer. Funny and moving, this film can help discussions of wishes for medical treatment and end-of-life care.

Related Movies and Animated Films

Big Fish (2003 – PG-13, 2 hr. 5 min.) A son returns home to be with his dying father during his last days. The father has told fanciful tales throughout his life, and the son struggles to determine fact from fiction. Raises issues of medical treatment, facing mortality, and family relationships; and shows a tear-inducing fantasy funeral. Directed by Tim Burton, it stars Ewan McGregor, Albert Finney, Billy Crudup, and Jessica Lange.

The Big Lebowksi (1998 – R, 1 hr. 57 min.) The only reason this comedy film is included here is the unfortunate death of bowling team member Theodore "Donny" Kerabatsos. The Dude and Walter Sobchak go to a funeral home to arrange for his cremation, followed by a famous ash-scattering scene (what not to do). The rest of the film is filled with curse words and a crazy crime story. Yet, this classic cult film, starring Jeff Bridges, John Goodman, Steve Buscemi, and Julianne Moore, may have a place in a festival.

The Bucket List (2007 – PG-13, 1 hr. 37 min.) Two very different terminally ill men head off on a road trip with a wish list of to-dos before they die. Features discussions of mortality, life and love, and cremation wishes. Stars Jack Nicholson and Morgan Freeman.

Coco (2017 – PG, 1 hr. 45 min.) This Oscar Award-winning animated adventure focuses on Miguel, a young aspiring musician, who is confronted with his family's ancestral ban on music. He enters the Land of the Dead to find his great-great-grandfather, a legendary singer. Illustrates the rich traditions of *Dia de los Muertos* in Mexico and Central America and shares a warm message about remembering our ancestors.

Death Becomes Her (1992 – PG-13, 1 hr. 44 min.) A comedy/fantasy that features "frenemies" who both get the same immortality treatment. Themes of eternal youth, beauty, and living forever compared to the benefits of living with a deadline can be discussed. Stars Meryl Streep, Bruce Willis, and Goldie Hawn.

Defending Your Life (1991 – PG, 1 hr. 52 min.) In this comedy/fantasy, at an afterlife way station resembling a major city, the lives of the recently deceased are examined in a court-like setting. Provides a fun way to start a discussion about reincarnation and what might happen to us after we die. Stars Albert Brooks, Meryl Streep, and Rip Torn.

Inside Out (2015 – PG, 1 hr. 35 min.) This animated comedy/adventure focuses on the emotions inside our heads and the impact they have on how we live. Follow young Riley as she is uprooted from her Midwest life and moved to San Francisco. Her emotions – Joy, Sadness, Fear, Anger, and Disgust – conflict on how to best navigate a new city, house, and school. Provides a profound lesson on the importance of recognizing and honoring loss and sadness.

The Seventh Seal (1957 – Not Rated, 1 hr. 36 min.) In this classic black-and-white film by director Ingmar Bergman, Max von Sydow plays a knight returning to Sweden after the Crusades. He seeks answers about life, death, and the existence of God as he plays chess against the Grim Reaper during the Black Plague. It's a great conversation starter about life and death philosophical issues. Dialogue is Swedish with English subtitles.

This is Where I Leave You (2014 – R, 1 hr. 43 min.) After their father dies, four grown siblings are forced to return to their childhood home and live under the same roof for a week as they sit *shiva*. Shows complicated family relationships, impacts of grief, and a bit about Jewish funeral traditions. Stars Jason Bateman, Adam Driver, Tina Fey, and Jane Fonda.

Waking Ned Devine (1998 – PG, 1 hr. 31 min.) This comedy focuses on the quirky residents of a tiny remote town on the Isle of Man and the lottery madness that ensues when Ned Devine's numbers come up – and he dies. Features a lovely scene that suggests the benefit of holding a living funeral. Stars Ian Bannen and David Kelly.

Documentaries about Death and End-of-Life Issues

Being Mortal (2015 – Not Rated, 54 min.) In this PBS FRONTLINE episode, Dr. Atul Gawande, author of the book of the same name, explores the relationships doctors have with patients who are nearing the end of life. The film investigates the practice of caring for the dying and shows how many doctors are untrained, ill-suited, and uncomfortable talking about chronic illness and death with their patients.

Consider the Conversation: A Documentary on a Taboo Subject (2011 – Not Rated, 60 min.) Consider the Conversation examines multiple perspectives on end-of-life care and includes information and experiences gathered from interviews with patients, family members, doctors, nurses, clergy, social workers, and national experts on death and dying.

How to Die in Oregon (2011 – Not Rated, 1 hr. 47 min.) In 1994, Oregon became the first state to legalize a terminally ill person's request to end his or her life with medication. This documentary follows several individuals through the issues and emotions surrounding terminal illness and the right-to-die movement.

Jack Has a Plan (2022 – Not Rated, 1 hr. 13 min.) When Jack, a man with a terminal brain tumor for 25 years, decides to end his life, his family and friends struggle to accept his decision. Jack's best friend documents his three-year quest to die a happy man.

Living While Dying (2017 – Not Rated, 45 min.) Filmmaker Cathy Zheutlin follows several people facing terminal diagnoses and making the most of the rest of their lives. The personal film is an invitation to have essential deep conversations as we re-imagine our own inevitable endings.

Patient: A Surgeon's Journey (2014 – Not Rated, 1 hr. 11 min.) Cardio-thoracic surgeon, Dr. Jeffrey Piehler, takes us through an exploration of being diagnosed with cancer, embracing life, and accepting mortality from his own experiences, first as a doctor and then as a patient.

Solace: The Wisdom of the Dying (2008 – Not Rated, 1 hr. 24 min.) This documentary grew from Camille Adair's experiences as a hospice nurse working with patients, families, hospitals, and cancer treatment centers. It offers a rich blend of perspectives on death as a natural and sacred human process rather than as a medical failure.

A Will for the Woods (2014 – TV-G, 1 hr. 33 min.) This documentary follows Clark Wang as he pursues green burial for his final disposition as he faces an untimely terminal illness. A powerful exploration of the environmentally beneficial act of choosing a green burial and the importance of facing one's own mortality.

For additional presentation options, check out film clip-illustrated presentations on specific topics in Chapter Eleven: "More from Gail Rubin."

Chapter 9

Marketing Guide

Planning Approach

As a festival organizer, I recommend using a dedicated journal or notebook to keep track of all your contacts and their replies. This list will include contacts made to sponsors, speakers, event locations, ideas for activities and anything else related to your festival. Write the date for each entry. Write down names, phone numbers and emails, company names and titles, and short summaries of the result of the interaction. This information all in one book, in physical form, can keep you organized and on top of the many moving parts of a **Before I Die Festival**. It's also a helpful record for creating subsequent festivals.

If you're a fan of spreadsheets, create an Excel spreadsheet to track your contacts to potential sponsors and partners. Columns can include the person's name, title, company, phone number, and email, and space for notes about each contact you make. Note the dates of emails sent, messages left, conversations held, and results of your outreach. Schedule dates for follow-up contacts in your calendar, so a promised action doesn't fall through the cracks.

Use a large wall calendar to plot out a multi-day event. Post it where you can see the ongoing development of the festival. This visual reinforcement of what is happening when can help you schedule a smooth flow of events, for both the organizers and the attendees. During meetings with other festival team members, a calendar can ensure everyone is "on the same page."

Planning Timeline

It's possible to pull a festival together in as little as four months, but you might want to work on a longer timeline for your own sanity. This flexible timeline includes creating festival events, working with sponsors, marketing/PR/advertising, and follow-up activities.

One Year to Six Months Ahead

- Identify festival dates and possible locations.
- Create your sponsorship proposal.
- Connect with sponsors and partners and secure their support.
- If working with a local movie theater, get events on their schedule.
- Create the festival website and build related social media accounts.

Six to Four Months Ahead

- Arrange for event locations.
- Schedule events and speakers.
- Continue to secure sponsors and partners.
- If using an online event management app, engage those services.
- Create marketing materials: logos, postcards, brochures, flyers, print and online advertisements, and additional artwork. Explore advertising placements in monthly/weekly publications.
- Write and send news release announcement to longer lead local outlets, such as monthly and weekly magazines.
- List event on tourism event calendars for your area.
- List events on your website as they are scheduled.

Four to Three Months Ahead

- Distribute marketing materials through partners, senior and community centers, and other locations where your target market of baby boomers and millennials gather.
- Continue working with sponsors, partners, and presenters to spread the word about the festival.
- Fine-tune event schedule and activities.
- Activate online registration forms, offer early bird registration discounts.
- Use a national news distribution service to announce the festival.

Three to Two Months Ahead

- Contact local newspapers and TV stations for advance news stories to promote event.
- Start online promotion boosting event posts to targeted audience on Facebook.
- Start posting on additional social media channels: Instagram, Twitter, LinkedIn, TikTok.
- Post festival events to local online calendars (CitySpark, NextDoor, Patch, Events.com, EventBrite.com, AllEvents.in). Boost as your budget allows.

Eight Weeks Ahead

- Mail postcards to target market of baby boomers and millennials encouraging participation in festival events.
- Send a weekly email update on developments to registered attendees, speakers, sponsors, and partners up to the start of the festival.
- Begin social media promotion of festival events with link to registration form.

Six Weeks Ahead

- Contact local radio and TV stations for interview opportunities.
- Contact local newspapers/print/online news media to generate advance stories about the upcoming festival.
- Continue weekly email update on developments to registered attendees, speakers, sponsors, and partners.
- Continue social media promotion of festival events with link to registration form.
- Investigate advertising opportunities in local media outlets including radio and newspapers.

Four Weeks Ahead

- Record and post promotional videos to YouTube encouraging festival registrations. This can include messages from participating speakers.
- Continue weekly email update on developments to registered attendees, speakers, sponsors, and partners.
- Continue social media promotion of festival events with link to registration form.

Three Weeks Ahead
- Send promotional messages for festival presenters to use to promote their participation on social media and encourage more registrations.
- Continue weekly email update on developments to registered attendees, speakers, sponsors, and partners.
- Continue social media promotion of festival events with link to registration form.
- Locations hosting events can post banners/signs promoting the upcoming festival.
- Keep Festival website updated with any changes to the schedule.

Two Weeks Ahead
- If holding hybrid online sessions, have technical rehearsals with each session presenter to ensure the best audiovisual connections, smooth use of slides or video, and answer questions about how the session will run. Usually takes less than 30 minutes per session.
- Hold live sessions on social media with presenters.
- Re-contact local news media for interviews and advance stories.

One Week Ahead
- Continue weekly email update on developments to registered attendees, speakers, sponsors, and partners.
- Continue social media promotion of festival events with link to registration form
- Hold live sessions on social media with presenters.
- Connect with local news media interviews for advance stories on radio, TV, and print.

Festival Time
- Keep count of how many people participate in each session, both in-person and online, to track numbers for the final report.
- Continue contacting local news outlets to encourage coverage of festival events.
- Take lots of interesting pictures of all festival elements and share on social media to encourage more people to join upcoming festival sessions.
- Make videos with presenters and record comments from festival attendees. Have all who record videos sign release forms allowing use of the videos.

Post-Festival Follow-up

- Send thank you notes to speakers, sponsors, partners, and participants.
- Edit and post videos of festival sessions on YouTube if you created videos.
- Survey festival attendees – see questions to ask under Post-Event Evaluation and Report in Chapter Seven: "Before I Die Festival Event Logistics."
- Write and send report to sponsors and partners – see topics to cover under Post-Event Evaluation and Report in Chapter Seven: "Before I Die Festival Event Logistics."

Chapter 10

Sample Before I Die Festival Materials and Forms

In this chapter, you will find helpful sample materials from different **Before I Die Festivals**, including postcards, a sample schedule, and drawing forms. Included are several documents that you can adapt to use for your festival. These Word documents are available by email upon request to **Gail@AGoodGoodbye.com**:

- A festival press release template in Word.
- The 10-page planning form from *A Good Goodbye: Funeral Planning for Those Who Don't Plan to Die*.
- Bare Bones Checklist for collecting information to create an Upon My Death letter.
- A helpful PDF overview of the Death Cafe's history, ground rules, and conversation-starting quotes.
- A speaker release agreement template for video recordings of Festival sessions.

Press Release Template

In the following press release template, simply replace the words in *italics* and (parentheses) with your local event details. For a shorter news release, you can omit the extra information about daily highlights.

Press Release Template (Continued)

Contact:
(Name)
(Phone)
(Email)

Before I Die *(location)* Festival *(dates)*
What's on Your Bucket List Before You Die?

(Location, Date) -- Have you thought about what you'd like to do before you die? Many people reflect on this question by creating a bucket list of goals and experiences they'd like to achieve during their lifetimes. If the Before I Die *(location)* Festival on *(dates)* isn't on your list, add it now! With ## events focused on death awareness and planning for end-of-life issues, this festival needs to be on everyone's bucket list.

The Before I Die *(location)* Festival offers creative activities and events that spur conversation around our inevitable mortality. The goal is to help people think and talk openly about death and dying in an upbeat space and take steps to plan ahead. Highlights include

- *(List 3-5 attention-getting events)*
- *Highlight*
- *Highlight*

See the full schedule of events and register online at *(festival website address)*.

"*(Quote by local organizer or sponsor about the importance of the event and how fun it will be.)*"

(List special speakers at the festival you'd like to highlight.)

Attendees at each festival event can enter a drawing to win *(list specific prizes)*.

(Optional added details) Must-See Events: Before I Die *(Location)* Festival

Press Release Template (Continued)

The *(year)* Before I Die *(Location)* Festival will be held in *(location of city/cities)*. Here's a snapshot of just a few daily scheduled events. Most events are free or low-cost if food is provided:

Day One Highlights *(date)*
- *(examples)* Panel discussion title *(speakers, location, time)*
- Death Cafe conversation *(details)*
- Cemetery tour *(details)*

Day Two Highlights *(date)*
- *(examples)* Behind-the-scenes funeral home tour, location, time
- Movie *(title & short description)*, location, time
- Workshop on obituary writing *(details)*

Day Three Highlights *(date)*
- *(examples)* Tour the Office of the Medical Investigator - see how real-life death investigations take place in *(location)*. *(details)*
- Hospice medical aid-in-dying conversation. *(details)*
- Symposium with ## sessions on topics such as *(list topics)*, *(details)*.

(Add more daily highlights as needed).

Festival sponsors include: *(list sponsors with links to websites, either alphabetically or in order of amount of sponsorship package)*.
- *Sponsor Name, website*
- *Sponsor Name, website*
- *Sponsor Name, website*
- *Sponsor Name, website*
- *Sponsor Name, website*
- *Sponsor Name, website*
- *Sponsor Name, website*

For the full schedule of events, registration form, speakers, and other information about the Before I Die *(Location)* Festival, visit *(festival website address)*.

A Good Goodbye Planning Form

Use this planning form to write down key information for your eventual Good Goodbye. If you've downloaded the electronic form from **AGoodGoodbye.com**, you can type into the form and save it as a new file. Or simply print out the document and write the details on the paper. Consider doing a separate form for each adult in your household. Feel free to expand this document as needed.

A Good Goodbye Planning Form

The Big Stuff Needed for a Death Certificate in the U.S.
(Includes The Five Things You Need to Know NOW Before Someone Dies)

Full Name (official first, middle and last on birth certificate):

Nickname (what your friends usually call you):

Maiden Name (if female):

For Jews – Hebrew Name:

Date of Birth (month/day/year):

Place of Birth (city and state or foreign country):

Social Security Number:

Residence Address (street, city, state, zip):

Sex:
(male or female – sorry, most death certificates don't have transgender options)

Father's Full Name:

For Jews – Father's Hebrew Name:

Mother's Full Maiden Name (better know this!):

For Jews – Mother's Hebrew Name:

Marital Status (check one):
__ single __ married __ divorced __ widow/widower

Surviving Spouse's Name (if wife, maiden name):

Served in U.S. Armed Forces (yes or no):

Preferred Method of Disposition:

Race:
(there is a space on death certificates for this)

Highest level of education:

Usual occupation:
(kind of work during career):

A Good Goodbye Planning Form (Continued)

Veteran Information (Thanks for your service! We salute you.)

    Location of DD214 Form:

    Service/Branch:

    Date and Place of Enlistment:

    Date of Discharge:

    Rank and Service Number:

    Veterans' Administration Claim Number:

    War/Conflicts/Tours of Duty:

    Commendations Received:

Marital History

    Current Marriage (to name and date):

    Previous Marriages (Names, dates of wedding and divorce finalization, or death date), current address and phone number of ex, notes):

Religious Information

    If you're "spiritual but not religious," atheist, or agnostic, consider writing down contacts for friends or a funeral celebrant you'd like to conduct a memorial service and where you'd like it held.

    Religion:

    House of Worship:

    Address and Telephone:

    Clergy to Contact:

Codes, Combinations and Online Passwords

    Mark down usernames and passwords for key online activities. Remaining live online after your demise can become a target for hackers and a problem for your survivors. Note other codes or combinations needed to access important information. You may want to create a spreadsheet or note if passwords are written in a log book and its location.

    Computer log-on or administrative access:

    Internet Service Provider:

    Email Provider:

    Facebook Account:

    Twitter Account:

A Good Goodbye Planning Form (Continued)

    LinkedIn Account:

    Instagram Account:

    Pinterest Account:

    TikTok/Other Accounts:

    Cell Phone Account:

    Burglar Alarm Code/Password:

    Online Banking/Investment Accounts:

    Online Merchant Accounts (i.e. Amazon, catalogues, stores):

    Web Site(s) Administration:

    Safe Combination:

    Other Accounts:

Family to Notify

    When time is of the essence, can you easily assemble the names, addresses, emails, and phone numbers for all your family and friends? *The Family Plot File* is an electronic data resource that will make contacting your family and friends so much easier and help smooth the way to a successful event. Download your copy today online through **https://agoodgoodbye.com/to-die-for-shopping/**. For each as applicable, enter name, city/state, telephone, email, and notes.

    Spouse:

    Parent:

    Parent:

    Child:

    Child:

    Child:

    Child:

    Child:

    Grandchild:

    Grandchild:

    Grandchild:

    Grandchild:

    Grandchild:

    Grandchild:

    Sibling:

    Sibling:

A Good Goodbye Planning Form (Continued)

Sibling:

Sibling:

Friends and Others to Notify

Name, Telephone, Email:

Name, Telephone, Email:

Name, Telephone, Email:

Name, Telephone, Email:

Name, Telephone, Email:

Name, Telephone, Email:

Name, Telephone, Email:

Name, Telephone, Email:

Name, Telephone, Email:

Name, Telephone, Email:

Name, Telephone, Email:

Name, Telephone, Email:

Executor (Name, address, telephone, email):

Digital Executor – if different from Executor (Name, address, telephone, email):

Insurance Agent/Company (Name, address, telephone, email):

Attorney (Name, address, telephone, email):

Financial Advisor/CPA (Name, address, telephone, email):

Other Professional Advisors (Name, address, telephone, email):

Obituary News Bits

In addition to helping draft an informative obituary, these details can be used to notify other people who will want to know about the death. If you want help preparing a great obituary, contact Gail Rubin to discuss her obituary writing services: **Gail@AGoodGoodbye.com**.

A Good Goodbye Planning Form (Continued)

Education

Include name of school, city and state, degree earned, dates attended.

High School:

Community College or Trade School:

University:

Graduate Degree(s):

Membership in Alumni Association(s):

Career Highlights

Note companies worked for and dates, achievements, awards, etc.

Hobbies and Interests

Note any pursuits or passions that play a large role in life.

Organizations to Contact

This is helpful to alert people who may be involved in your professional, community, or volunteer life. This can include unions, fraternal organizations, professional interest groups, volunteer services, and other community contacts. List the name of the organization, website, address, telephone, and, if possible, a specific contact person. If no longer a member, you may want to note the dates of membership. Note if you'd like to name one of these organizations as a memorial donation beneficiary.

Organization:

Organization:

Organization:

Organization:

Organization:

Organization:

Newspapers or Publications for Obituary

List the local newspapers or trade publications that would be appropriate for either a paid obituary announcement or a news obit. Having the publication name, telephone, and website address handy is one less stressor during a trying time.

Publication:

Publication:

A Good Goodbye Planning Form (Continued)

Publication:

Publication:

Document Locator

Let your family know where the important documents are kept. Here's a quick run-down of what documents and other information your family will need to put their hands on if there's a medical emergency or death. Note "yes or no" regarding each piece, where it's located, an account number or other reference as needed, and any other notes.

Will:

Living Will:

Living Trust:

Medical Power of Attorney:

Durable Power of Attorney:

Cemetery Plot Deed:

Veteran DDE 214 Form:

Body/Organ Donor Information:

Safe Deposit Box:

Safe Deposit Box Key:

P.O. Box:

P.O. Box Key:

Automobile Title(s):

Birth Certificate:

Passport:

Divorce Papers:

Life Insurance:

Health Insurance:

Long Term Care or Disability Insurance:

Auto/Home Insurance:

Savings Accounts:

Checking Accounts/Checkbooks:

Credit Cards (account #s, toll-free phone):

Annuities:

Mortgage Papers/Deeds:

A Good Goodbye Planning Form (Continued)

    Income Tax Records:
    Retirement Plans:
    Government Benefit Statements:

Your Final Wishes

Sketch out what you envision for your Good Goodbye. Fill in responses as appropriate.

Preneed arrangements made:
(if yes, name funeral provider and contact info)

Preneed funding done (if yes, name company and contact info):

Travel insurance for return of body, if purchased:
(company, phone, and contract number)

Disposition of remains (burial, cremation, donation of body, other):

Prefer a funeral (body present) or a memorial service:
(cremains or not present)

Prefer a wake, viewing, picnic, wild party, other gathering:

If donating to science or medical school, list arrangements:

Cremated remains:
(bury, scatter, keep in urn, columbarium, share with family, other options)

Cemetery plot or mausoleum crypt purchased (list section, block, plot):

Casket preference (material and price range):

Open or closed casket:

Embalming preference (yes or no):

A Good Goodbye Planning Form (Continued)

Clothing, jewelry, other burial item preferences (such as eyeglasses):

Marker preference (headstone or plaque):

What do you want on your tombstone?

Location of funeral/memorial service:

Favorite flowers:

Memorial gifts in lieu of flowers:

Officiating clergy or friends:

Speakers – eulogy and readers:

Readings:

Music selections, musical instruments, performers:

Casket bearers:

Honorary pallbearers:

Location of prepared obituary:

Other special instructions:

"Bare Bones" Planning Checklist

Want to help ease the burden on your loved ones who will have to deal with your inevitable demise, without having to undertake too much work? Write down these key pieces of information. This can apply to you or someone else you want to plan for.

"Bare Bones" Planning Checklist

Death Certificate Details

Write down your full name, Social Security number, date of birth, city of birth, parents' full names, including mother's maiden name, and military service details, if applicable. All of this information is required on a death certificate.

Who To Call Contacts

List the most important family and friends to call with their phone numbers and email addresses. Also write down professionals, such as your financial advisor, attorney, insurance agent, and executor.

Important Information Locator

Let your loved ones know where to find your will or trust (if you have one), Power of Attorney documents, insurance policies, preneed funeral plans, and the DD214 form for veterans' benefits. Write down computer, phone, and online passwords for accounts and social media. Include information on mortgages or loans, credit cards, bank accounts, utilities, retirement pension, and other financial accounts.

Your Valuables

List valuable items you own. Even if you don't own homes or cars, there may be valuables to appraise and distribute – jewelry, musical instruments, artwork, furniture, books, coin or stamp collections, and other items.

Death Details

At the very least, state your disposition preference – burial, cremation (by fire or water), donation to science, or body composting. If you preplan and prepay with a funeral home, or you own burial plots, put that paperwork with your other important papers.

Ideas about how you would like people to celebrate your life after you are gone will be appreciated more than you may realize. But don't be bossy – people need the latitude to mourn your loss as they see fit.

"Bare Bones" Planning Checklist (Continued)

If you want to "flesh out" this "bare bones" checklist with more details for your loved ones, visit **www.AGoodGoodbye.com** to download a free 10-page planning form. It's from Gail Rubin's book, *A Good Goodbye: Funeral Planning for Those Who Don't Plan to Die*. Or you can request the form with an email to **Gail@AGoodGoodbye.com**.

Remember, talking about sex won't make you pregnant and talking about funerals won't make you dead.

Death Cafe Information Handout Example

(Can insert logo for local festival)

Welcome to the Before I Die Festival Death Cafe!

What to expect:
- We'll start out introducing ourselves and what drew us to this event, then branch into discussion.
- It is a casual cafe environment, no formal breaks. If you gotta go, get up and go!
- If you feel overwhelmed and need to step out, that's okay, too.

The principles we follow:
- The event is *free from ideology* – It is against Death Cafe principles to lead participants towards any conclusions about life, death, or life after death, apart from your own thoughts.
- The event should *feel safe and nurturing*, which includes offering nice refreshments.
- The event is accessible and *respectful of all*, regardless of gender orientation, religion/faith, ethnicity, and disability.
- The event is *confidential*. No individual stories should be retold without approval.

Conversation starters:

What brought you here today?
How would you complete the statement: Death is_____.
What factors in your life lead you to feel about death the way that you do?
What contradictions do you have in your own thoughts about death?
Before I die, I want to_____.
Which quote most resonates with you (see following quotes)?

Quotations to ponder:

1. *Death ends a life, not a relationship.* – Mitch Albom, *Tuesdays with Morrie*

2. *I'm not afraid of death; I just don't want to be there when it happens.* – Woody Allen

3. *Everyone wants to go to heaven, but nobody wants to die.* – Joe Louis

4. *What a more beautiful world this would be if we didn't wait till people were dead before we honored their spirit.* – Kellie Elmore

5. *Life is pleasant. Death is peaceful. It's the transition that's troublesome.* – Isaac Asimov

Death Cafe Information Handout Example (Continued)

6. *I want to die in my sleep like my grandfather... Not screaming and yelling like the passengers in his car.* – Will Shriner

7. *If life is a school, loss is a major part of the curriculum.*
   – Elisabeth Kübler-Ross

8. *I'd rather rot on my own floor than be found by a bunch of bingo players in a nursing home.* – Florence King

9. *When someone is born, we rejoice. When someone is married, we celebrate. But when someone dies, we pretend that nothing happened.* – Margaret Mead

10. *Die before you die, so that when you die, you will not die.*
    – Egyptian Book of the Dead

11. *When we finally know we are dying, and all other beings are dying with us, we start to have a burning, almost heartbreaking sense of the fragility and preciousness of each moment and each being, and from this can grow a deep, clear, limitless compassion for all beings.*
    – Sogyal Rinpoche, *The Tibetan Book of Living and Dying*

12. *The only cure for your suffering is to lean into the source of its pain.*
    – Celtic Book of the Dead

13. *I learned early to keep death in my line of sight, keep it under surveillance, keep it on cleared ground and away from any brush where it might coil unnoticed.* – Joan Didion

14. *A man dies as many times as he loses a loved one.* – Syrus

15. *All architects want to live beyond their deaths.* – Philip Johnson

16. *Death is a very dull, dreary affair, and my advice to you is to have nothing whatsoever to do with it.* – W. Somerset Maugham

17. *Death is the last enemy: Once we've got past that I think everything will be all right.* – Alice Thomas Ellis

18. *Do not fear death so much but rather the inadequate life.* – Bertolt Brecht

19. *No one can confidently say that he will still be living tomorrow.* – Euripides

20. *The fear of death follows from the fear of life. A man who lives fully is prepared to die at any time.* – Mark Twain

For information about Death Cafe events worldwide,
please visit **www.DeathCafe.com.**

Press Release Example

FOR IMMEDIATE RELEASE
May 13, 2019
Contact: Dan Katz
PH: (800) 991-0625 ext. 1
Email: dkatz@laadsmarketing.com

"Before I Die" – Bakersfield Festival Celebrates Life and Death

Day-long event to be held at Greenlawn Southwest on Saturday, June 1.

Bakersfield, CA – Death almost always seems to be a surprise. That's why most people are woefully unprepared when it happens. The "Before I Die" – Bakersfield Festival, taking place on Saturday, June 1, 2019 at Greenlawn Memorial Park Southwest in Bakersfield, will help people plan ahead for their 100% guaranteed mortality with a variety of death-discussion-friendly events.

Gail Rubin, Certified Thanatologist and The Doyenne of Death®, an award-winning author and TEDx speaker, is the featured presenter at the festival. According to Rubin, by taking even a few small steps, you can reduce the stress, conflict and confusion death causes. It starts with simply talking about death in the open.

"Just as talking about sex won't make you pregnant, talking about death won't kill you," said Rubin.

"This festival gives people a chance to find out everything they always wanted to know about death, funerals, cremation and burial but were always afraid to ask," said Jim LaMar, president of Greenlawn Funeral Homes and Cemeteries. "We want to take the fear out of thinking about death and funerals and maybe even inject a bit of entertainment into the day."

"Before I Die" Festivals and Death Café events are now cropping up around the country and drawing large numbers of attendees. The Bakersfield event will take place at Greenlawn Southwest, 2739 Panama Lane, Bakersfield on June 1 from 10 am to 7 pm, and will conclude with a showing of the movie "Undertaking Betty," a romantic – sometimes outrageous –

Main address: 3700 River Blvd. Bakersfield, CA 93305 • (661) 324-9701 • www.GreenlawnM-C.com

Press Release Example (Continued)

comedy with a behind-the-scenes look at two funeral homes in a small Welsh village, featuring Alfred Molina, Naomi Watts and Christopher Walken. The film begins at 5 pm. All events are free.

The schedule of events includes these activities:

- "Death Café" conversation preceded by The Newly-Dead Game® that allows everyone in the audience to play along, answering questions about wills, final disposition preferences, advance medical directives, and thoughts on a final resting place. The game prompts questions and conversations in a fun, upbeat way.
- Outdoor "Mortuary Mall," features caskets, urns, cremation jewelry, and other funeral/memorial products and services for attendees to examine and ask questions of knowledgeable staff.
- Crematory tour includes a talk by a cremation expert explaining the process and answering questions people have about scattering, environmental impact, creative things people do with cremated remains, and other issues.
- Mortuary tour takes guests into the "Authorized Personnel" areas of the mortuary to shine a light on what happens behind the scenes.
- Estate Planning and End-of-Life Issues: local estate planning experts and attorneys will answer people's questions about the financial and legal aspects of planning ahead.
- "How Do You Want to be Remembered?" is a panel discussion on obituary writing, ideas on how to leave one's life story for future generations and wording for memorial markers.
- "Laughing in the Face of Death: Funny Films for Funeral Planning:" Gail Rubin's keynote speech incorporates comedy film clips to illustrate the importance and benefits of preneed funeral planning.

Main address: 3700 River Blvd. Bakersfield, CA 93305 • (661) 324-9701 • www.GreenlawnM-C.com

Press Release Example (Continued)

- "Everything You Always Wanted to Know About Death **But Were Afraid to Ask*" brings together a panel that includes a funeral director, a hospice caregiver, clergy and other experts to field questions from the audience.
- "The Woo-Woo Side of Death" features a fun conversation on ghosts, afterlife, near-death experiences and the paranormal.

The full schedule of events will be available online at www.GreenlawnM-C.com. Food and refreshments will be available at the event.

Main address: 3700 River Blvd. Bakersfield, CA 93305 • (661) 324-9701 • www.GreenlawnM-C.com

Media Advisory Example

MEDIA ADVISORY AND PRE-EVENT INTERVIEW OPPORTUNITY

"Before I Die" – Bakersfield Festival Celebrates Life and Death
Day-long event to be held at Greenlawn Southwest on Saturday, June 1.

What: This unusual end-of-life festival gives community residents a chance to find out everything they always wanted to know about death, funerals, cremation and burial but were always afraid to ask. The event is free. (Festival program on following pages.)

Who: Gail Rubin, Certified Thanatologist and The Doyenne of Death®, an award-winning author and TEDx speaker, is the featured presenter at the festival. Also nationally recognized psychic medium Tammy Holmes, will keynote a panel on "The Woo Woo Side of Death." Other speakers throughout the day will talk about financial planning, hospice care, obituary writing.

Where: Greenlawn Southwest - 2739 Panama Ln, Bakersfield, CA

When: Saturday, June 1 from 10 am to 7 pm

Why: The intention is to take the fear out of thinking about death and funerals and maybe even inject a bit of entertainment into the conversation. There has never been an opportunity in Kern County for the public to get "up close and personal" with a funeral home or cemetery, outside of dealing with a death. This opens the doors and lets in the air on an otherwise frightening subject.

Pre-Event Interview Opportunities: Festival co-organizer, Gail Rubin, The Doyenne of Death®, is available by phone or Skype in advance. She can be reached at (505) 363-7514 or Gail_Rubin@comcast.net. Jim Lamar, president of Greenlawn Funeral Homes and Cemeteries, can be reached at (661) 324-9701 or jamesl@greenlawnm-c.com.

Media Contact: Dan Katz
PH: (800) 991-0625 ext. 1
Email: dkatz@laadsmarketing.com

Main address: 3700 River Blvd. Bakersfield, CA 93305 • (661) 324-9701 • www.GreenlawnM-C.com

Festival Schedule Example

Before I Die Festival

Everything you ever wanted to know about getting ready for The End

Saturday, June 1, 10am - 7pm
Greenlawn Southwest

Upbeat, offbeat, we're putting the "fun" into funeral planning

With a 100% chance of mortality, the Bakersfield "Before I Die" Festival fosters reflection about how we address death and dying. By providing space and opportunities to openly discuss end-of-life issues and learn from experts, we can improve the outcome of the actions we take to prepare for our mortality. All Festival events are free and open to the public.

Program Schedule

10 am - 5 pm — **Mortuary Mall** - Welcome, door prizes, caskets, urns and other products on display in the Celebration of Life parking lot.

10 am - 11:30 — **"The Newly Dead Game"/Death Café** - Conducted by The Doyenne of Death®, Gail Rubin, the audience plays along, answering questions about wills, final disposition preferences, advance medical directives, and thoughts on a final resting place. Expect surprises. Following is our Death Cafe, where death, cookies, tea and coffee make for interesting and even entertaining conversation.

11:45 am - 12:15 pm* — **Crematory Retort Tour** - A talk by a cremation expert explaining the cremation process up close and personal. Questions about scattering, environmental impact, creative things people do with cremated remains, and other issues will be answered. (*Also repeated at 1:30 and 3 pm.)

12:30 pm - 1* — **Mortuary Tour** - What's behind those closed doors? We'll open them up and show you, and answer ALL your questions, from embalming to casketing, and more. Nothing is off limits. (*Also repeated at 2:15 and 3:45 pm.)

Workshops & Panels

What You Should Know about Hospice Care - Hospice experts talk about this significant and humane end-of-life choice, including medical aid in dying.

1 pm - 1:45 repeated at 3 pm - 3:45 — **Laughing in the Face of Death** - Funny Films for Funeral Planning: Gail Rubin's keynote speech incorporates comedy film clips to illustrate the importance and benefits of preneed funeral planning.

Obituary Writing & Being Remembered - Workshop and discussion on how you want to be remembered and various ways to preserve your life story for future generations, from text to online. A life story writing guide will be provided.

MORE EVENTS & PROGRAMS ON OTHER SIDE

FREE COMMUNITY EVENT

Festival Schedule Example (Continued)

Program Schedule - continued

Workshops & Panels

Estate Planning / End of Life Issues - Work with local financial planners and attorneys to answer questions about wills, trusts, probate, estates and everything else that gets left behind.

2 pm - 2:45 repeated at 4 pm - 4:45

The "Woo-woo" Side of Death - Paranormal experts, ghost hunters and psychics talk about what's on the "other side," communicating with the dead, Near Death Experiences (NDEs) and haunted Bakersfield. Are you a believer, a skeptic or just curious?

Everything You Always Wanted to Know about Death, *but were afraid to ask* - We've assembled a fantastic panel that includes a funeral director, a hospice caregiver, and clergy to field any and all questions from the audience. Greenlawn's own Jim LaMar is moderator.

5 pm - 7

Movie: "Undertaking Betty" - Undertaking Betty (2002 PG-13) is a romantic comedy with a behind-the-scenes look at two funeral homes in the small village of Wrottin-Powys in Wales. This funeral film offers a fun way to start funeral planning conversations by showing both traditional and highly outrageous personalized send-offs. Popcorn? Oh, of course!

"Remember: Talking about sex won't make you pregnant. Talking about funerals and end-of-life issues won't make you dead."
— Gail Rubin, CT

Festival coordinator and Doyenne of Death®, Gail Rubin, CT, is a pioneering death educator who works with companies to connect with baby boomers concerned about end-of-life issues. A featured speaker at TEDxABQ in 2015, she's the author of three books on end-of-life issues, including *A Good Goodbye: Funeral Planning for Those Who Don't Plan to Die* and *KICKING THE BUCKET LIST: 100 Downsizing and Organizing Things to Do Before You Die*. She's also a Certified Funeral Celebrant. In a previous lifetime, she was a public relations professional and an event planner. Learn more about Gail at www.AGoodGoodbye.com.

Greenlawn Southwest
2739 Panama Lane, Bakersfield, CA 93313

Sponsored By

Greenlawn
FUNERAL HOMES
CREMATIONS • CEMETERIES

Northeast: **(661) 324-9701**
Southwest: **(661) 834-8820**
Online: **www.GreenlawnM-C.com**

A Friend of the Family℠

Voted Best Funeral Home 11 Years in a Row

Greenlawn Southwest FD# 1347, Greenlawn River Blvd FD# 779
© 2019 Greenlawn. A Friend of the Family is a trademark of Dan Katz, Inc.

Prize Registration Form Example

Prize Registration

Fill out ALL information to win assorted door prizes, including **ground interment for two, cremation fountain niche for two**, free vault and interment on two funeral plans, free flower arrangement from our floral cabinet, and books by Gail Rubin.

Please PRINT clearly.

Name _____

Address _____

City _____ State _____ Zip _____

Phone _____ Age _____

Email _____

The information you provide us above is to notify you if you won any prizes. Further, we may from time to time contact you with information about our services. If you would like to opt out of our contacting you (other than winning notification), please check the box here. ☐

How did you hear about this event? (Check all that apply)

Brochure/Flyer_____ Email_____ Friend_____ Facebook_____

Web Site _____ Newspaper_____ Radio_____ TV_____

Other (Specify)_____

Greenlawn
FUNERAL HOMES
CREMATIONS • CEMETERIES

A Friend of the Family®

Speaker Release Agreement Example

You can type out this speaker release agreement and tailor it for your own organization/company and festival events. Make sure to put your own company name in and the correct date/year.

SPEAKER RELEASE AGREEMENT

THE UNDERSIGNED, _____ ,
(Print)

Residing at _____
(Full address)

in the county of _____, State of _____ hereby agrees and consents to grant *Company Name* the absolute and irrevocable right and permission to use my name and likeness to: reproduce, edit, exhibit, project, display, copyright, publish the moving pictures and/or videotaped images of me with or without my voice, or in which I may be included in whole or in part, photographed, taped, videotaped and/or recorded and to circulate the same in all forms of *Company Name* projects and/or any other lawful purpose whatsoever. It is acknowledged that I have agreed to waive compensation for such consent and that no other compensation is required. By this consent, I waive any and all claims that may exist in connection to the above.

THIS AGREEMENT is executed on this _____ day of _____, 2023.

_____
(Signature)

_____
(Phone number)

_____
(Email)

Local Festival Proposal Example

Connect with Baby Boomers and their Millennial Children: Before I Die NM Festival
October 30-November 2, 2021

"This festival has something for EVERYONE who is interested in end-of-life issues. Great speakers, great topics, great opportunities for participation. I highly recommend it!"

— *2020 Festival Participant*

The coronavirus pandemic brings mortality issues to top-of-mind awareness. The 5th annual **Before I Die New Mexico Festival, October 30 to November 2, 2021** can help end-of-life-related businesses connect with the public. The festival will combine virtual and in-person events in Albuquerque (as local health guidelines permit) that can be shared in other markets.

SPONSOR BENEFITS:

Reach both baby boomers and millennials through pioneering death educator, speaker and author **Gail Rubin, Certified Thanatologist**. Thanatology, the study of death, dying and bereavement, offers important post-pandemic insights. Since 2010, Rubin's properties, *A Good Goodbye* and *Before I Die Festivals*, have connected sponsors and partners to baby boomers and their millennial kids. She can introduce these consumers to your products and services, drive sales and grow your customer base.

ABOUT THE FOUNDER: GAIL RUBIN

Gail Rubin, CT, puts the "fun" in funeral planning while connecting organizations with potential customers. She was one of the first people to host a Death Cafe in the United States and is a leading advocate for planning ahead. An award-winning TEDx speaker, she's the author of three books on end-of-life issues, including *A GOOD GOODBYE: Funeral Planning for Those Who Don't Plan to Die* and *KICKING THE BUCKET LIST: 100 Downsizing and Organizing Things to Do Before You Die*.

Albuquerque Business First named Gail one of their **2019 Women of Influence**. In a previous lifetime, she was a public relations professional and event planner. Her motto: "Just as talking about sex won't make you pregnant, talking about funerals won't make you dead."

Contact - PH: 505.265.7215 Email: Gail@AGoodGoodbye.com
P.O. Box 36987, Albuquerque, NM 87176-6987
Get updates at WWW.AGOODGOODBYE.COM AND WWW.BEFOREIDIEFESTIVALS.COM

Local Festival Proposal Example (Continued)

Connect with Baby Boomers and their Millennial Children: Before I Die NM Festival
October 30-November 2, 2021

These 2020 Before I Die *Virtual* Festival Sponsors have received 27,000+ YouTube views since the four-day online Festival:

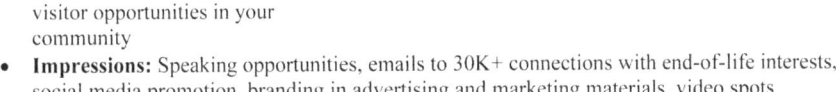

PARTNER BENEFITS INCLUDE:

- **Visibility:** Branding to attendees, YouTube viewers, national resource list, website logos
- **Access:** On-site exhibitor and visitor opportunities in your community
- **Impressions:** Speaking opportunities, emails to 30K+ connections with end-of-life interests, social media promotion, branding in advertising and marketing materials, video spots
- **Connections:** Contacts of attendees, local partners for programming

WHO ATTENDS:

The **Before I Die New Mexico Festival** entices baby boomers and millennials to face their own mortality with festival events that educate and encourage planning for the inevitable. Contacts are collected through online registration to access virtual and in-person festival events.

- **Baby boomers**, a demographic of **78.2 million**, are turning 65 at a rate of 10,000 people **every day** through 2029.
- They have money to spend, with assets totaling $59.4 TRILLION, 70% of disposable income in the U.S.
- This Silver Tsunami is about to crash on the shore of mortality.
- Lifelong agents of change, baby boomers want to be educated about end-of-life issues.
- Their **millennial** children, **79.5 million** people ages 24 to 40, comprise an even larger population wave.
- Millennials are digital natives, entirely comfortable conducting online research and financial transactions.
- Less than 30% of adults do any end-of-life planning!

Previous New Mexico in-person festivals drew 600 participants in 2017, 685 in 2018, and 1,800 in 2019. **In 2020, the combined audience for virtual live and recorded sessions was 27,000 and growing.** The International Cemetery, Cremation and Funeral Association (ICCFA) recognized the 2018 NM Festival with their KIP Award for Best Event.

Contact - PH: 505.265.7215 Email: Gail@AGoodGoodbye.com
P.O. Box 36987, Albuquerque, NM 87176-6987
Get updates at WWW.AGOODGOODBYE.COM AND WWW.BEFOREIDIEFESTIVALS.COM

Local Festival Proposal Example (Continued)

Connect with Baby Boomers and their Millennial Children: Before I Die NM Festival
October 30-November 2, 2021

PROGRAM DETAILS:

Festival events will take place in-person in Albuquerque and online in a Zoom meeting room. Both in-person and virtual sessions get post-event exposure as YouTube videos with sponsor/partner credits. *Other markets can be involved with in-person events teamed up with the virtual online events.*

Events include speakers, expert panel discussions, short films, a Halloween party, and more:
* **Death Cafe** discussions in-person or online, an opportunity to discuss mortality questions.
* **Tours** of sponsors' locations and discussions of products or services.
* **"Millennial Morticians with ABQ Brews,"** a panel discussion by young funeral professionals.
* **Informative Speakers** – sessions on obituary writing, estate and financial planning, death and the afterlife, history and new trends in death care, grief and more.

ULTIMATE MARKETING PLAN:

The Festival and its sponsors and partners will be promoted through the following channels:

- Emails to a combined total of 35,000+ subscribers to Gail Rubin's emails and the Reimagine end-of-life festival platform (www.LetsReimagine.org).
- Social media postings and ads for events & sponsor shares.
- Public relations to generate broadcast interviews and print/online news stories about the Festival.
- Print and radio advertisements in selected New Mexico publications and stations.
- Online calendar of event listings boosted in New Mexico.
- Short videos promoting festival events will be posted on YouTube, Facebook, LinkedIn, Twitter, and Instagram (12,000+ followers combined).

CHARITABLE PARTNER:

Part of the proceeds from the **Before I Die NM Festival** will be donated to Albuquerque-based charitable partner Historic Fairview Cemetery. The cemetery, founded in 1881, is the final resting place for approximately 12,000 people. An outdoor history museum, notable people who influenced the development of Albuquerque, New Mexico and the United States are buried here. This 501(c)(3) nonprofit organization maintains the grounds and shares the history through educational events. A portion of sponsorship fees may be tax-deductible.
www.HistoricFairviewCemeteryABQ.org

Contact - PH: 505.265.7215 Email: Gail@AGoodGoodbye.com
P.O. Box 36987, Albuquerque, NM 87176-6987
Get updates at www.AGoodGoodbye.com and www.BeforeIDieFestivals.com

Local Festival Proposal Example (Continued)

Connect with Baby Boomers and their Millennial Children: Before I Die NM Festival
October 30-November 2, 2021

Before I Die NM Festival Partnerships

The **Before I Die New Mexico Festival** gives partners the opportunity to grow their businesses with baby boomers and millennials. A customized program will be created for every partner, and you'll receive a detailed report after the event.

Partnership Level	Investment	Benefits	Multi-Benefits Package
Crystal Sponsor	$Level 1	• Visibility • Access • Impressions	• Assistance creating your local in-person event schedule. • Access to NM Festival virtual sessions to show in-person or online for partner events. • Hyperlink to partner website from AGoodGoodbye.com, with 30,000 unique visitors monthly, and BeforeIDieNM.com. • Recognition on Before I Die Festivals Facebook Page. • Partner recognition & links in press releases.
Ruby Sponsor	$Level 2	• Visibility • Access • Impressions • Connections	*All of the benefits from the Crystal level plus:* • Partner receives contact information for registrants at every event. • One online speaking opportunity or video tour of partner's location/service. • Partner Festival presentations that are recorded can be edited and posted on YouTube with other Festival videos.
Emerald Sponsor	$Level 3	• Visibility • Access • Impressions • Connections • Direct Response	*All of the benefits from the Ruby level plus:* • A partner video spot at the beginning of each Festival session video posted to YouTube. • Attendees can receive special offers to drive customers to your company's products and services. • Two virtual video tours/presentations or online presentations recorded and posted on YouTube. • Option to provide a prize for a drawing that draws attention to partner's products/services.

Contact - PH: 505.265.7215 Email: Gail@AGoodGoodbye.com
P.O. Box 36987, Albuquerque, NM 87176-6987
Get updates at WWW.AGOODGOODBYE.COM AND WWW.BEFOREIDIEFESTIVALS.COM

Local Festival Proposal Example (Continued)

Connect with Baby Boomers and their Millennial Children: Before I Die NM Festival
October 30-November 2, 2021

Gail Rubin, as seen in and heard on:

Kiplinger Money THE HUFFINGTON POST

Books by Gail Rubin:

"Gail is about the only person I know that can make the subject of dying and death and funerals actually palatable."
— Larry Ahrens,
Radio & TV
Broadcast Host

Present and Past Sponsors and Clients

This is a great opportunity to join this prestigious group of sponsors who have already partnered with A Good Goodbye and Gail Rubin in reaching the lucrative baby boomer market on end-of-life issues in a fun, upbeat series of presentations and events. Please contact us and connect your brand with the profitable, growing number of boomers and their families.

Call now and join in the success! 505.265.7215

Contact - PH: 505.265.7215 Email: Gail@AGoodGoodbye.com
P.O. Box 36987, Albuquerque, NM 87176-6987
Get updates at WWW.AGOODGOODBYE.COM AND WWW.BEFOREIDIEFESTIVALS.COM

Festival Announcement Examples

Post card examples from the **Before I Die New Mexico Festival**. These were designed for distribution at locations rather than for mailing.

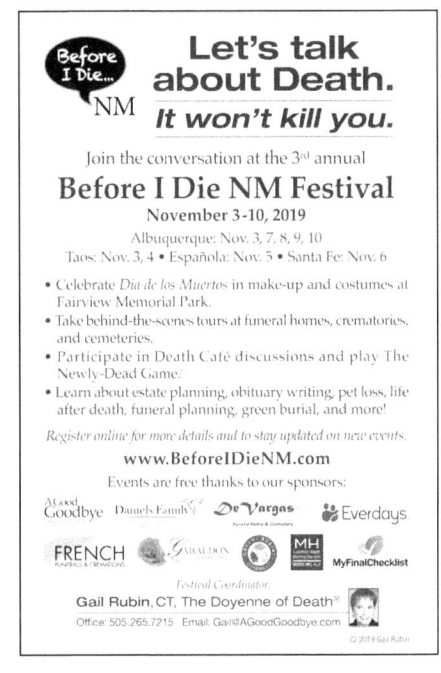

Chapter 11

More From Gail Rubin

The Before I Die Festival in a Box™

The **Before I Die Festival in a Box** is available in two forms: as a stand-alone book that provides guidance on how to hold a festival, and in a box with additional items that can be used for festival activities. The book is distributed through IngramSpark, with global distribution to independent bookstores, online stores including Amazon.com, eBook retailers, and libraries. The additional items included in the box with the book are only available through **www.BeforeIDieFestivals.com**.

The additional elements in the **Before I Die Festival in a Box** include:

- *A Good Goodbye* TV interview series on preneed planning. The four-DVD set contains twelve 30-minute interviews covering funeral planning, cremation, cemeteries, financial and estate planning, green burial, grief, funeral celebrants, pet loss, green burial, and more. Episodes can be shown as part of festival events.

- **Newly-Dead® The Game** is a fun way for couples to learn how well they know each other's last wishes. It's like the old TV game show, *The Newlywed Game*. All you need to add are large pads of paper and Sharpie® markers for players to write down their answers. Or play the four-question singles' version to test everyone's preparedness. Offer prizes for participants that will help reinforce learning about and undertaking end-of-life planning. A digital version of both the couples and singles' games can be purchased and downloaded at **www.AGoodGoodbye.com**.

- **Newly-Dead® Bingo** gamifies teaching about end-of-life issues. The playing cards have 25 squares with words that list different aspects of death, and a free space in the center. As each item is called, the emcee can provide helpful tips that educate players as the game progresses. 50 game cards, instructions, and a list of definitions of terms are included.

- In addition, you get one hour of consulting time to help you get your festival up and running.

Film Clip-Illustrated Presentations

To pack a lot of information with entertaining film clips about funeral and end-of-life issues into a 60- to 90-minute time frame, consider some of these film clip-illustrated presentations. Audiences remember lessons illustrated by movie scenes better than just the words of a speaker. I have a license to legally use films and TV shows in my talks. Presentation topics include:

- **Laughing in the Face of Death: Funny Films for Funeral Planning**
  This upbeat talk illustrates funeral planning issues with clips from comedy films and television programs. Learn what you need to know before someone dies to reduce stress and conflict, save money, and create a "good goodbye." Just as talking about sex won't make you pregnant, talking about funerals won't make you dead – and your family will benefit from the conversation.

- **Answers to Your Burning Questions on Cremation**
  — a.k.a. Ashes to Ashes, Dust in Your Face
  Cremation is the fastest growing disposition method in the U.S. Watching funny and serious film clips, learn about what you need to know about cremation before there's a death in the family, including choices to make and disposition options.

- **We Can Do That? New Trends in Death Care**
  — a.k.a. Green/Natural Burial Options
  The modern funeral is changing. Learn about new death care trends in

the United States, including green burial, DIY/home funerals, alkaline hydrolysis, and other developing body disposition methods, rising cremation rates, and how to make a memorial service all about the person who died.

- **"Doctor, How Long Do I Have?"**
Having a serious healthcare conversation with your doctor and family takes effort to ensure clear communications. Learn how to ask questions and be involved in treatment decisions by watching dramatic and comedy films depicting doctor-patient-family conversations.

- **Going Home: Taking Death Out of the Hospital**
Even though 75% of Americans say they want to die at home, fewer than 25% of us do. Using comedic and serious movie clips, learn about ways to de-medicalize our final days. Really – you can laugh about death while learning about the benefits of hospice.

- **The Many Faces of Grief: Mourning in the Movies**
The process of grief and mourning takes on many faces. Using clips from Hollywood films to illustrate and lighten the conversation, learn about different grieving styles, tips for managing mourning, and other insights from thanatology, the study of death, dying, and bereavement.

- **Jewish Funeral Traditions on Film**
Did you know Jewish burial is naturally green burial? Jewish traditions regarding death and dying, the funeral, the treatment of the body, burial, mourning, and annual remembrances are very different from Christian practices. This talk illuminates the differences and similarities of these funeral traditions – highly beneficial for interfaith families.

- **The Funeral Director on Film**
Watching scenes from comedies and dramas focused on funeral directors throughout history, learn the history of U.S. undertaking, perceptions of funeral directors and funeral planning tips. With humorous insights, Gail Rubin educates and entertains with Hollywood portrayals of "the last man to let you down."

Other talks based on the TV series *The Kominsky Method* and *Six Feet Under* are available. Additional film clip talks include **Hollywood's Visions**, **Trips** and **Crowded Rooms**, **On Choosing to Die**, **The Viking Funeral on Film**, and **Estate Planning: Hollywood Myth versus Facts**. For more information, visit **www.AGoodGoodbye.com**.

Speaking and Consulting

If you'd like guidance putting your **Before I Die Festival** together, one hour of consulting is included in the **Before I Die Festival in a Box** through **www.BeforeIDieFestivals.com**.

Would you like The Doyenne of Death® to present at your festival? Let's talk! You can reach me at 505-265-7215 or email **Gail@AGoodGoodbye.com**.

More About Gail

Gail Rubin, CT, The Doyenne of Death,® is author of the award-winning books *A Good Goodbye: Funeral Planning for Those Who Don't Plan to Die*, *Kicking the Bucket List: 100 Downsizing and Organizing Things to Do Before You Die*, and *Hail and Farewell: Cremation Ceremonies, Templates and Tips*. She is also the coordinator of the award-winning **Before I Die New Mexico Festival** and a pioneer of the Death Cafe movement in the United States.

A doyenne is a woman who is considered senior in a group who knows a lot about a particular subject. Gail is a Certified Thanatologist (a death and grief educator) and speaker who uses humor and films to get end-of-life conversations started. Her 2015 TEDx talk (**https://youtu.be/r9qR4ZiGX2Y**) focuses on the importance of starting end-of-life conversations before there's a death in the family. *Albuquerque Business First* named her one of their Women of Influence in 2019.

She hosts The Doyenne of Death® podcast and regularly posts videos on a range of end-of-life related topics to her YouTube channel, @GailRubin. She has been featured in *The New York Times*, *The Wall Street Journal*, NPR, PBS, *Kiplinger* and *Money* magazines and other news outlets.

Gail is a member of the Association for Death Education and Counseling (ADEC), the International Cemetery, Cremation and Funeral Association (ICCFA), Toastmasters International, and the National Speakers Association.

Her motto is: "*Talking about sex won't make you pregnant. Talking about funerals won't make you dead.*"

Learn more and sign up for a free planning form and Executor's Checklist at **www.AGoodGoodbye.com**.

Learn more about **Before I Die Festivals** at **www.BeforeIDieFestivals.com**.

www.ingramcontent.com/pod-product-compliance
Ingram Content Group UK Ltd.
Pitfield, Milton Keynes, MK11 3LW, UK
UKHW021309180426
11947UKWH00015B/1123